THEATRE CAFE

PLAYS TWO

T0347506

COMPANY OF ANGELS

Company of Angels was set up in 2001 by John Retallack to foster and produce innovative theatre for young audiences. The company's mission is to broaden the definition of theatre for young people through experimental projects and new productions of high artistic standard.

This publication brings together a second selection of highlights from Company of Angel's biannual Theatre Café Festival of new European writing for young audiences. *Theatre Café Festival 2010* will be held in association with Unicorn Theatre and Southwark Playhouse and will include *Blowing* by Jereon van den Berg directed by this year's *Young Angels Award* winners, Fanshen.

Artistic Director: John Retallack
Dramaturge: Teresa Ariosto
Producers: Vanessa Fagan/Virginia Leaver
Company Secretary: David Harris
Contact: www.companyofangels.co.uk
126 Cornwall Road, London SE1 8TQ
020 7928 2811
info@companyofangels.co.uk

Theatre Café

PLAYS TWO

JEROEN VAN DEN BERG

Blowing

Translated by Rina Vergano

ANJA HILLING

Sense

Translated by Logan Kennedy and Leonhard Unglaub

DARJA STOCKER

Nightblind

Translated by Philip Thorne

OBERON BOOKS

LONDON

This anthology first published in the UK in 2010 by Oberon Books Ltd
521 Caledonian Road, London N7 9RH
Tel: 020 7607 3637 / Fax: 020 7607 3629
e-mail: info@oberonbooks.com
www.oberonbooks.com

Visit www.oberonbooks.com to read more about all our books and
to buy them. You will also find features, author interviews and news
of any author events, and you can sign up for e-newsletters so that
you're always first to hear about our new releases.

Contents

Introduction

Theatre Café is about giving a platform to brilliant new European plays that have had considerable success in their own countries - but which have not been seen in the UK. Company of Angels have now commissioned seventeen new translations of plays that have received their first readings at Theatre Café.

Some of the plays have been written expressly for young people, some have simply caught the imagination of young people in their own countries.

WHAT IS THEATRE CAFÉ?

It is a theatrical space designed to create an informal, intimate atmosphere where audiences can relax and feel very close to a play. Every performance is followed by a discussion - often with the participating presence of the playwright. There's room for audience involvement and also for the writers to benefit from the process.

Theatre Café started in 2004 at the Arcola Theatre in Hackney. Twelve plays from nine European countries were read over two weeks in the special Theatre Café setting created by designer Liz Cooke.

The twelve plays were selected from among more than 150 submitted; none had been produced in the UK before and three were given their first English translations, commissioned by Company of Angels for Theatre Café.

The feedback suggests that we succeeded in creating the informal and intimate atmosphere that we wanted. Audiences were unanimous in saying that the scripts in the actors' hands were soon forgotten as they were drawn into the story, while the vast majority of teenagers expressed their love of the setting and of the opportunity to talk informally with actors, writers and directors after the show.

Ten of the twelve authors came over to take part in the event and in the debate. They were enthused by the possibilities offered by Theatre Café.

I didn't know what to expect from a staged reading but I must say that the Theatre Café performance went far beyond what I dared to hope for. The setting itself made a very good connection between audience and actors, and the play worked perfectly in this atmosphere even though it is written for smoke, flying characters and a revolving stage. I kind of forgot it was a staged reading; the papers in their hands became something like a concept rather than a reminder of words or text. Andri Snær Magnason (Iceland)

The simple set left space for imagination and many things were actually more effective in the reading than they would have been in a full production. Juha Jokela (Finland)

Company of Angels looks for European plays that are original in both form and style and with important stories to tell; they must also be plays that we believe speak to a wider public, beyond the immediate country of origin.

Following the success of the 2004 edition, Theatre Café went to a new level in 2007 with four major events going on simultaneously in four different parts of Europe - in London, in Tallinn, in Lille and in Amsterdam.

Company of Angels collaborated with VAT Teater (Estonia), MUZ Theater (Holland) and Le Grand Bleu (France) and together mounted staged readings of 20 new plays from all over Europe. All of the plays were heard for the first time in each respective language. Company of Angels installed Theatre Cafe at the Unicorn Theatre and, for the first time, we hosted an International Symposium.

I got some very positive feedback from directors. One of them wants to stage my play in Berlin, at the English Theatre. There are also requests from London. And just the other day the French translator for the Lille reading wrote that it went very well in France and asked if he can send it out to directors and publishing houses over there. This means Theatre Cafe works and plays circulate, which is always a great thing. I hope the project continues in the following years because there aren't so many like it. Stefan Peca (Romania)

After the Symposium, the Swedish Embassy invited Company of Angels to curate a special version of Theatre Café, in order to bring the most original and thought-provoking work being written in Sweden today to the attention of British producers.

Company of Angels has a long standing commitment to emerging artists whom we nurture through our Young Angels development programmes and our Angels Associates scheme.

In 2008 Theatre Café evolved as a festival, linking the company's work with emerging artists to its established European dimension and expanding to two different London venues, with readings taking place at the Unicorn Theatre and fully mounted productions at Southwark Playhouse. Southwark Playhouse and the Unicorn are neighbouring theatres in Tooley Street, SE1.

Angels Associates Mia Theil Have and Max Webster translated and directed *Sandholm* by Anna Bro; Philip Thorne and Oystein Brager of Imploding Fictions presented the Swiss play *Norway. Today* by Igor Bauersima – and 4 young directors presented extracts of *Invasion!* by Jonas Hassen Khemiri (translated by Frank Perry) competing for the first £20,000 Young Angels Theatremakers Award to direct a Theatre Café play. The award was won by Lucy Kerbel and her production took place at Soho Theatre in March 2009.

> *I think it was a very inspiring and well organised festival. You could feel that it had come to life out of a great passion and interest in theatre for young people. And a genuine wish to be inspired by theatre from outside England. The danger with international readings are, that they sometimes seem like a commercial for a country ("come buy Danish writing!") which is a bit weird to me. But this was pure love of theatre. Great! I came home with new polished international glasses. Ready to look a bit more out at the world.* Anna Bro (Denmark)

Theatre Café is now an established biannual event with the Symposium gathering representatives from all over the British theatre industry and beyond. The festival is unique because it brings European work and young theatremakers together, featuring each year the Young Angels Theatremakers Award winner and giving young directors the opportunity to show their talent.

With our 2010 programme we return to Unicorn Theatre and Southwark Playhouse, building on our success in 2008.

We have now succeeded in finding plays that British repertory theatres want to produce as a result of seeing them at Theatre Café.

The three plays published in the *Theatre Café Plays One* anthology, have all been produced in the UK between 2008 and 2010.

Of the plays in this volume, *Sense* has already received two productions in 2009 and 2010; *Blowing* is embarking on a national tour in 2010 and *Nightblind* is lined up for a London fringe production in 2011. Company of Angels is involved in these productions, either in an advisory capacity, or as a co-producer.

In 2010 we are presenting five new plays; the International Symposium chaired by Royal Court Literary Manager Chris Campbell; the Young Angels Award 2009 winner, *Blowing*, directed by Angels Associates Dan Barnard and Rachel Briscoe of emerging company fanSHEN; and a workshop presentation of a new British play, *Arlo* by John Retallack. We are also staging *Ank!Ang!*, a unique collaborative playwriting project about children, teenagers and adults from all across Europe, initiated by LABOO7 in Paris. Angel Associate Mia Theil Have will work with the Southwark Playhouse Young Company to direct episodes by playwrights from France, Sweden, Germany, Italy and Portugal and two specially commissioned episodes from Spain and the UK.

With ten productions of eight different plays, and four more in preparation, Theatre Café has become an indispensable way of moving plays and artists between different cultures and languages. We hope more and more European plays will be seen on UK stages in the near future and that we will play a part in that development through presenting a third Theatre Café Plays anthology at our 2012 festival.

Teresa Ariosto and John Retallack
Theatre Café Curators
(October 2010)

THEATRE CAFÉ PLAYS PRODUCED IN THE UK:

- *Truckstop* by Lot Vekemans (Holland), Edinburgh Festival and UK tour, 2007

- *This Child* by Joel Pommerat (France), Theatre Café Festival and UK tour, autumn 2008 and ALRA, London, spring 2010

- *Invasion!* by Jonas Hassen Khemiri (Sweden), Soho Theatre, London, spring 2009

- *Sense* by Anja Hilling (Germany), Southwark Playhouse, London, spring 2009 and Imaginate Festival, Edinburgh, spring 2010

- *Monsters* by Niklas Rådstrom (Sweden), Arcola Theatre, London, spring 2009

- *Respect* by Lutz Hübner (Germany), Birmingham Rep, spring 2010

- *Colors* by Peca Stefan (Romania), Tristan Bates Theatre, spring 2010

- *Blowing* by Jeroen van den Berg (Holland), Theatre Café Festival and UK tour, autumn 2010

- *Nightblind* by Darja Stocker (Switzerland), London Fringe, in preparation for spring 2011

- *Sandholm* by Anna Bro (Denmark), ALRA, in preparation for spring 2011

- *Anne and Zef* by Ad de Bont, National Tour, in preparation for spring 2012

THEATRE CAFÉ 2004

I Love This Country / Austria
by Peter Turrini translated by Zoe Svendsen (translation
commissioned by Company of Angels)

The Dreamed Life of Nora Schahrazade / Sweden
by Mia Törnqvist translated by May Brit Akerholt

Time of Darkness / Sweden
by Henning Mankell translated by Ann Henning Jocelyn

The Letter / Croatia
by Aleksander Miljkovic translated by Aleksander Miljkovic

Mother Africa / Holland
by Ad de Bont translated by Rina Vergano (translation
commissioned by Company of Angels)

Mausoleum / Hungary
by Lajos Parti-Nagy translated by John Batki

Encroachment / Czech Republic
by Iva Volankova translated by David Nykl

Truckstop / Holland
by Lot Vekemans translated by Rina Vergano

Rambo 7 / Iceland
by Jon Alti Jonasson translated by Jon Alti Jonasson

The Heart of a Boxer / Germany
by Lutz Hübner translated by Penny Black (translation
commissioned by Company of Angels)

Mobile Horror / Finland
by Juha Jokela translated by David Hackston

The Wild Children of the Blue Planet / Iceland
by Andri Snær Magnason translated by Andri Snær Magnason
and Julian Meldon D'Arcy

THEATRE CAFÉ 2007

Bats / Portugal
by Jaime Rocha translated by Alice de Sousa (translation commissioned by Company of Angels)

Blowing / Holland
by Jeroen van den Berg translated by Rina Vergano

Colörs / Romania
by Peca Stefan

Do you like Porn? / Sweden
by Klas Abrahamsson translated by Gabriella Berggren

The Real Elvis / Estonia
by Urmas Vadi translated by Liina Unt

Helver's Night / Poland
by Ingmar Villqist translated by Jacek Laskowski

In Memoriam / Belgium
by Hanneke Paauwe translated by Rina Vergano (translation commissioned by Company of Angels)

Invasion! / Sweden
by Jonas Hassen Khemiri translated by Frank Perry (translation commissioned by Company of Angels)

Respect / Germany
by Lutz Huebner translated by Zoe Svendsen (translation commissioned by Company of Angels)

So Young, So Blonde, So Totally Confused / Belgium
by Gerda Dendooven translated by Rina Vergano (translation commissioned by Company of Angels)

This Child / France
by Joel Pommerat translated by Nigel Gearing (translation commissioned by Company of Angels)

THEATRE CAFÉ 2008

Sense (Sinn) / Germany
by Anja Hilling translated by Logan Kennedy and Leonhard Unglaub

Nightblind / Switzerland
by Darja Stocker translated by Philip Thorne (translation commissioned by Company of Angels)

Bulger / Belgium
by Klaas Tindemans translated by Gregory Ball

Sandholm / Denmark
by Anna Bro translated by Mia Theil Have and Max Webster (translation commissioned by Company of Angels)

Headcase / Holland
by Esther Gerritsen translated by Rina Vergano (translation commissioned by Company of Angels)

THEATRE CAFÉ 2010

Anne and Zef / Holland
by Ad de Bont translated by Rina Vergano (translation commissioned by Company of Angels)

The Woods / Norway
by Jan Jesper Halle translated by Nicholas W. Norris

Dead Girls Don't Grow Up / Spain
by Beth Escudé i Gallès translated by John Ginman

Am I Comforting You Now? / Sweden
by Ann-Sophie Bárány translated by Edward Buffalo Bromberg (translation commissioned by Company of Angels)

Clyde and Bonnie / Austria
by Holger Schober translated by Zoë Svendsen (translation commissioned by Company of Angels)

COMPANY OF ANGELS
FUTURE AND PAST PROJECTS

Forthcoming productions and projects include: the new *Choreography for Children Award*, developed in partnership with Sadler's Wells and The Place: London Contemporary Dance School to encompass new choreographic work for young audiences; *Truant*, a research and development collaboration with the National Theatre of Scotland; two contemporary European plays to be co-produced in association with Academy of Live and Recorded Arts and Drama Centre, London. Between autumn 2010 and spring 2011 Company of Angels will co-produce a range of projects with the Bristol Old Vic Theatre.

Recent projects include: *Apples* by Richard Milward, an outstanding first book adapted by John Retallack, a co-production with Northern Stage and winner of an Edinburgh Festival Herald Angel Award; *Colors* by Peca Stefan (Romania) and *Tattoo* by Dea Loher (Germany) at Tristan Bates Theatre, London; *Iphigenia* by Pauline Mol (Netherlands) and *This Child* by Joël Pommerat (France) produced in association with ALRA, both contemporary European plays examining the nature of family relationships through classical and current settings; *Sense*, a series of 5 plays by the award winning author Anja Hilling, at Southwark Playhouse; *Children in Wartime*, three contemporary plays exploring this theme, produced in association with ALRA; and *Theatre Café Festival 2008*, our biannual new European writing festival in association with Unicorn Theatre and Southwark Playhouse.

The company not only produces shows but also initiates innovative projects and new models of work. *Theatre Café* and *Young Europe* have successfully brought new foreign plays to UK audiences; *Asylum Seeker Narratives* and its successor *Project R* are community schemes that directly involve young people; the *Gap Theatre Project*, a unique peer-mentoring initiative, has been expanded to include *Gap Theatre Project Teacher Training*. The next planned *Gap Theatre Project* will take place in summer 2011 in a north London primary school, working in partnership with Scarabeus Theatre and Islington Community Theatre.

Company of Angels also actively nurtures and supports emerging artists through the *Young Angels* programmes and the *Angels Associates* scheme.

Current publications available: *Theatre Café Plays One* (Oberon);

Company of Angels: Four Plays by John Retallack (Oberon); *Six Ensemble Plays for Young Actors* featuring *Sweetpeter* by John Retallack (Methuen); *Apples* by Richard Milward adapted by John Retallack (Oberon); *Theatre Café Plays Two* (Oberon).

Company of Angels has been a Regularly Funded Organisation of Arts Council England since April 2004.

BLOWING

Q&A with JEROEN VAN DEN BERG

Why do you write for the theatre?

I started writing for the theatre while I was on the directing course of the Drama Academy. I found it hard to find plays that I wanted to direct so I decided to try and write my own.

What does 'Europe' mean to you?

A very interesting likeness of totally different people and cultures. There are great opportunities for the people of Europe to work together without losing their respective identities. Beyond that, there's the bureaucratic aspect of Europe which is less interesting to me.

Do you think your play could work anywhere in the world?

I think my play could work in any Western country where people grow up in families like the Beumers.

How is *Blowing* relevant to your homeland?

I think a lot of children live in families like the Beumer family, with parents who try to hide the truth of their relationship from their children, causing damage to them all.

What is the significance of the roll-down shutters in relation to Dutch society?

We have an expression: don't show your dirty laundry to strangers. In Dutch society, it's common to hide your problems and give the outside world the image that you're totally happy. So the shutters prevent the outside world from seeing what's really happening inside the Beumer house.

What varied responses has the play sparked in audiences?

When the play is performed for children, Jurgen gets a lot of sympathy. Adult audiences often find the mother's behaviour horrible until they discover why she acts as she does. Audiences find the way that the Beumer family acts funny and horrible at the same time.

Do young people ever watch it with their parents or always on their own?

The play has been performed by various companies. Some of these are children's theatre companies which travel from school to school. Others perform the play for regular audiences in theatres. In those cases, there's a mixed audience of children and adults which I personally prefer.

SENSE

Q&A with ANJA HILLING

Why do you write for the theatre?

Because I am interested in the potential of the form to go beyond the limits of the stage.

Do you think your play could work anywhere in the world?

It's difficult to say. These are people, situations and conflicts that emerge from the needs of an affluent society.

How did the five senses structure come about?

The play was a commissioned work, five dialogues that are interpreted by drama students for performance in school classrooms. The requirement for five episodes and the dominance of the body in adolescence gave me the idea of the senses.

Was this play driven by a particular perspective on love and relationships?

No.

What do you feel for the individual characters in *Sense*?

I tried to imagine what it is like to be young today. That was difficult for me. In the end I gave up and didn't search anymore for a language and habits of youth but instead based my writing more on eternal wishes and fears – love, acceptance, death, guilt, freedom – all of these things. Then they all grew close to my heart.

Could you comment on the language of the play and the process of writing it?

For this play I thought a lot about narration – two people meeting each other and looking for words – how to find a language for this. How different is their perception of each other, of themselves and of the world? A story is told as if it were already over but then the present breaks into the narration again and again; a dialogue, a situation, a touch.

Are you happy to see individual episodes performed or would you rather see the play performed as a whole?

I think there is a lot of potential in both ideas

NIGHTBLIND

Q&A with DARJA STOCKER

Why do you write for the theatre?

I am interested in understanding people emotionally, to look at them in a way that I rarely get the opportunity to in real life. Through theatre I can observe how a character acts in specific situations and through the language I can share their deep feelings, their pain, their hope and their doubts.

Do you think your play could work anywhere in the world?

I think everybody around the world now has the feeling of being dependent on someone, of not being honest to his/her self, the feeling of losing their identity and personality in a desperate situation. The play is situated in the middle classes and it focuses on the lack of communication between parents and adolescents, and also between the mother and father. I can imagine that the specific observations I make about this class might seem strange to an audience in a country where other family structures and hierarchies exist.

What inspired you to write this play?

I was not inspired; I felt dejected by the knowledge of what happens to women that I considered emancipated, independent and full of self-awareness. I saw that emancipation and equality exists in the language of many people but that it is not evident in their actions.

I also wanted to write this play because as a girl and a young woman I found that violence as an aspect of adolescence was something which was often played down. For me it was terrible, because adults didn't take the victims seriously, and sometimes neither did the adolescents who where dealing with violence. I observed a sort of lack of communication between the young generation and the older generation, with the older generation seemingly afraid of problems and not able to provide a caring opposition to the problem.

Did you do any research in order to write this play?

I found the theme accidentally. When I decided to write a play about it, I searched for women whose lives had been affected by the theme and I found many.

What governed your choice of dramatic form and structure?

I was impressed and touched by the way the young women talked about their experiences. Their inner position changed a lot while they were speaking and they realised this but they could not recognize or analyse what had happened between them and their boyfriend. So for the theatre I thought it would be interesting to see this ambivalence in which they were captured. That's how I decided to have Leyla speak in monologues instead of having violent scenes on stage with her boyfriend. I was more interested in the inner motivation of the woman to stay or leave, her fight with herself.

The language between Mo and Leyla is very tight. As adolescents they don't have many words to explain their pains and problems; because it would hurt too much and they don't recognize the causes yet, because of the dependence on parents, school, and the whole situation. Mo can't admit his dream because the consequences would hit him too hard...

How would you like to have affected your audience by the end of the performance?

I wanted to show that it is always possible to find consciousness again, if someone is open to a new situation and is able to see himself how he or she could be. I wanted to say: another kind of relationship with someone else, but also with one's self, is possible. But everybody has to choose his way out for him/herself.

What would you hope for Leyla and Mo?

That they should find out what is good for them, fight for it and follow their inner wishes.

BLOWING

Jeroen van den Berg
Translated by Rina Vergano

Further Copyright Information

Characters

FATHER

MOTHER

ESTHER

JURGEN

Translator's note:

NAMES

The names of the characters in the play are typical Dutch names, as in the original version of Blowing. *Names of characters are sometimes shortened in the dialogues to a single syllable: Esther to Es, Jurgen to Jurg and Thea to Thee.*

English names can be substituted throughout if so desired.

FIRST PERFORMED IN THE UK DURING COMPANY OF ANGELS' THEATRE CAFÉ EUROPE SEASON (9 – 21 OCT 2007).

Blowing was commissioned by Bas Zuiderland of Het Laagland in Sittart

It is a beautiful sunny day. The whole family is dressed for a party. The table is laid with an exaggeratedly lavish brunch. Father is fiddling about with the control panel of a roll-down security shutter system, JURGEN is reading and ESTHER is sitting at the breakfast table, Mother is standing in front of the window, on the telephone.

MOTHER: Fantastic. No, really fantastic darling. Marvellous day. Forty-five my foot. Don't feel a bit like it *(Laughs very loudly)*. It's a party, *(To children and father.)* it's party-time round here isn't it guys –

FATHER: *(Reading the operating instructions.)* 'Insert the key into the control panel and enter your code' –

MOTHER: I feel marvellous. It's only a number after all, forty-five.

FATHER: Jurg-

MOTHER: Do you remember when mother turned forty-five. She was already old then. Grey dresses and orthopaedic shoes – exactly – Look at me, it's a question of different times Thea, I'll get to a hundred at least –

FATHER: Jurg-

MOTHER: They're going to make all kinds of discoveries you watch – That's not optimistic, that's realistic.

FATHER: I can't see a code anywhere Jurg.

MOTHER: There's no reason for me to be pessimistic at all. It's terribly jolly round here. I've put together a fantastic brunch. Been preparing it for days.

FATHER: Jurg-

ESTHER: Just stop reading Jurg.

JURGEN: *(Imitates her, as he reads on.)* Just stop reading Jurg.

MOTHER: You should see it. Us sitting here all together. Leo's got a new suit, he's even wearing a bow-tie, I finally talked him into it Thee *(Laughs)*.

FATHER: Here. It says: your code. *(Tugs at his bow-tie.)*

MOTHER: Leave it alone Leo, it looked fine as it was – well he was fiddling with it, no no, looks wonderful on him, really suits him. What do you mean by that Thee. He looks marvellous in it –

ESTHER: Mummy-

27

MOTHER: Hang on Thea, Esther's saying something –

ESTHER: Are we going to eat or what –

MOTHER: *(To Esther.)* I'm just talking to auntie Thea – You should see us sitting here Thee. Leo with that bow-tie and Jurgen, Jurg's doing really well at school, got his nose in a book all day long, so studious – And Esther. Turning into a real little lady. I was walking along the street with her the other day Thee, they thought we were sisters, didn't they Es-

ESTHER: It happened once-

MOTHER: Can you hear, she says so herself, Es, tell auntie Thea-
(Passes her the telephone.)

ESTHER: *(Doesn't take the telephone.)* Are we going to eat or what.

FATHER: *(Still engrossed in his operating instructions.)* This is completely unintelligible.

MOTHER: *(Into the telephone.)* That's just what I mean. Forty-five my foot. It's how you feel that counts. And I feel fantastic. They're so sweet to me Thea, table laid, piles of presents – I'm not trying to say anything – I'm just describing what I see Thea-

FATHER: *(Slams his hand down on the operating instructions.)* I don't understand a word of this! Jurg!

JURGEN: Do you have to do it on her birthday.

FATHER: You watch: install these shutters tomorrow and they'll be on the doorstep tonight, those burglars.

MOTHER: What do you mean, no, I'm only saying-

JURGEN: What is there to steal here?

FATHER: Hey hey, we're very well off. Have a look round. And then just add it all up.

MOTHER: Listen Thee, I wasn't trying to say anything-

ESTHER: Who says the burglars are specifically coming today.

FATHER: You can hear them riding round on their scooters every evening. They've been watching us for weeks. *(Meanwhile looking at the operating instructions.)* I just don't understand- *(Presses buttons randomly.)*

MOTHER: We are happy here yes, is that my fault.

FATHER: *(Shouts.)* Oh for Christ's-

MOTHER: Do that later Leo.

FATHER: I'm nearly there Els!

MOTHER: Leo's in the middle of installing security shutters.

FATHER: *(Hits the control panel, shouts.)* This is bloody
unintelligible! *(The shutters roll down, it becomes dark in
the room.)*

MOTHER: Leo!

FATHER: Ah-ha!

JURGEN: I can't read like this.

ESTHER: Dad!

FATHER: I said I was nearly there.

MOTHER: Leo! Hang on Thee- I'm suddenly sitting in the dark. Leo!
I've got to go Thee *(Hangs up.)*

FATHER: Brilliant!

MOTHER: I'm not celebrating my birthday like this Leo!

FATHER: What's the matter?

MOTHER: Open those shutters!

FATHER: *(Lights a lighter, tries to read the instructions.)* Ehm-

JURGEN: *(Turns a lamp on.)*

FATHER: Hang on everyone-

MOTHER: You managed to make them go down just now.

FATHER: So?

MOTHER: So you can make them go up again.

FATHER: I fail to see the connection Els.

MOTHER: You are so bloody impractical, you're so bloody bloody-
(She gets up.) I'm not sitting here waiting in the dark.
(Exits briefly, comes straight back.) There's a security
shutter over the front door Leo!

FATHER: You wanted the whole house made secure.

MOTHER: I wanted to keep them out.

FATHER: Exactly.

MOTHER: This is the other way round. I can't get out of my own
house!

FATHER: If you just calmly-

MOTHER: I can't stand it Leo. Can't you try to make one day nice for me. A pleasant day just once a year- Is that too much to ask?

FATHER: *(Reading instructions.)* I just haven't quite cracked it.

MOTHER: Haven't quite cracked it. *(goes and stands behind him.)* Raise these shutters Leo.

FATHER: Don't stand over me Els, it makes me bag of nerves!

MOTHER: *(Grabs at the key on the control panel.)*

FATHER: Get off, you can't just - *(the shutters rolls upwards.)*

MOTHER: So simple Leo-

FATHER: How did you do that.

MOTHER: Okay. The day is already ruined. Thanks to Leo Beumer.

ESTHER: Can we eat now.

MOTHER: Forget it. After a start like that it's a dead loss. I won't let my birthday be spoilt by anyone.

FATHER: But Els just listen-

MOTHER: Nothing of the sort. We'll just start all over again and don't you lay a finger on these security shutters Leo.

BLACK OUT

*It is a beautiful sunny day. The whole family is dressed for a party. The table is laid with an exaggeratedly lavish brunch. **FATHER** is reading the newspaper, Jurgen is reading too and **ESTHER** is sitting at the breakfast table, bored. **MOTHER** is standing in front of the window, on the telephone.*

MOTHER: Fantastic. No, really fantastic darling. Marvellous day. Forty-five my foot. Don't feel a bit like it *(Laughs very loudly)*. It's a party, *(To children and father.)* it's party-time round here isn't it guys –

FATHER: *(Towards the telephone.)* Yeah it's party-time round here Thea- *(JURGEN gives his father a mocking look.)* Well it is isn't it-

MOTHER: I feel marvellous. It's only a number after all, forty-five. Do you remember when mother turned forty-five-

ESTHER: Mum-

MOTHER: She was already old then. Grey dresses and orthopaedic
shoes – exactly – Look at me, it's a question of different
times Thea, I'll get to a hundred-and-fifty at least –

They're going to make all kinds of discoveries you watch
– That's not optimistic, that's realistic.

ESTHER: Mum-

MOTHER: You should see it. Us sitting here all together. Leo's got a
new suit, he's even wearing a bow-tie, I finally talked him
into it Thee *(Laughs, FATHER tugs at the bow-tie).*

ESTHER: Just stop reading Jurg.

JURGEN: *(Imitates her, as he reads on.)* Just stop reading Jurg.

MOTHER: Leave it alone Leo, it looked fine as it was –

ESTHER: Dad-

FATHER: *(Doesn't react.)*

MOTHER: Well he was fiddling with it, no no, looks wonderful on
him, really suits him. What do you mean by that Thee. He
looks marvellous in it –

ESTHER: Mummy-

MOTHER: Hang on Thea, Esther's saying something – *(To ESTHER.)*
I'm just talking to auntie Thea-

ESTHER: Are we going to eat or what –

FATHER: *(From behind his newspaper.)* We're waiting for you Els.

MOTHER: *(Into the telephone.)* Leo says hello- That's just what I
mean. Forty-five my foot. It's how you feel that counts.
And I feel fantastic. They're so sweet to me Thea, table
laid, piles of presents – I'm not trying to say anything
– I'm just describing what I see Thee- what do you mean,
no, I'm only saying- listen Thee, I wasn't trying to say
anything- No-we are happy here yes, is that my fault.
You're not no, but it's my birthday, I don't feel like listening
to your problems on my- I just don't feel like it- *(To
JURGEN who is putting a slice of bread on his plate.)* Just
wait till I'm finished. I'm terribly sorry Thea, but I feel fine,
I feel young and I've got a fantastic family- *(Furious.)* It
didn't fall into my lap at all, we've all worked damned hard
at it- Yes that is what I think yes- You are in control of a
very large part of your own happiness yes- If you'd just

tried a bit harder- You had your chances Thee, you got off to an even better start than me- Eric had money-

FATHER: *(Looks up from his newspaper.)*

MOTHER: That's not unkind, it's just the way I see it. Eric had money when you married and your children are much cleverer than mine- I'm very happy with Jurgen and Esther but they're not brilliant, whereas your children-

JURGEN: *(Starts singing.)* Happy birthday to you, happy-

MOTHER: I can't hear if you sing Jurg- They're singing for me Thee, they can't wait any longer, I've really got to- You can hear them singing can't you- they were just singing, Jurgen-

JURGEN: *(Reads his book intensely.)*

MOTHER: I'm talking to you Jurg- (Into the telephone.) You must have heard him singing just now, listen Thee, I've still got a whole pile of presents to open (Meanwhile straightening **FATHER**'s bow-tie.), there's a magnificent brunch on the table- no, not breakfast, it's a brunch- well that's just what it is, listen Thee, I really have to- (brushes a lock of hair out of Esther's eyes, Esther brushes the lock straight back.) I know- (puts her hand over the receiver, whispers to Esther.) Let's sing happy birthday again darling-

ESTHER: Are we going to eat or what-

MOTHER: Just sing first. *(Starts singing, **ESTHER** joins in.)*

> Happy birthday to you, Happy birthday- *(Into the receiver.)* Thee, they really want me to come to the table now- I'm coming guys- *(Sings.)* to you, happy birthday dear- *(Into the receiver.)* I've really got to hang up now Thee, bye then- *(Hangs up.)* That woman thinks-

FATHER: And- *(Leads singing.)* For she's a jolly good fellow – *(**ESTHER** and **JURGEN** join in.)*

MOTHER: You can stop now guys- Leo- Leo please stop- Jurgen- She's already hung up. *(The song ends.)* It's absolutely unbelievable, she's completely self-centred.

ESTHER: I'm hungry-

FATHER: *(Holds up a present for **MOTHER**.)* Happy birthday!

MOTHER: She just can't stand the fact that other people are having a good time.

FATHER: *(Still holding the present.)* Look Jurg!

Hang on Es. Present first- *(Puts the present in front of* **MOTHER** *on the table.)* Els-

MOTHER: She can't stand it, she just can't stand it.

FATHER: *(To* **JURGEN**, *pointing to the present.)* Hey Jurg, look over here-

ESTHER: Open it mum-

MOTHER: She didn't even say happy birthday I don't think. *(Unwrapping her present.)* Damn. She didn't even say happy birthday! I sincerely hope we never get like that. Putting others first, that's so important guys, but she doesn't realise that, does she, and that's why it went wrong with uncle Eric-

FATHER: Jurg, look here-

MOTHER: He has a lot to put up with, doesn't he, uncle Eric?

JURGEN: Uncle Eric is a boring git.

MOTHER: Nonsense. You've always been mad about uncle Eric haven't you Es- But no-one can put up with that, in the long term, a woman like that drives away everyone around her. It's true isn't it Leo. A woman like that- (as if she gets given a video camera every day.) Oh, a video camera, how nice- (keeps talking as she unwraps it.)

FATHER: See Jurg, a video camera-

MOTHER: She needn't bother phoning me again Leo, if she's going to be like that.

FATHER: Hey Jurg, broadcast quality eh.

MOTHER: Don't know what I've done to deserve it.

FATHER: There's a tape with it too Els. *(Hands her a tape.)*

MOTHER: *(Looks through the lens.)* I can't see a thing though.

FATHER: There must be some instructions somewhere-

JURGEN: *(Removes the lens-cap from the lens.)*

MOTHER: Ah yes-

ESTHER: Can we eat now-

FATHER: Hang on, we've got to get a recording first. Hey Jurg, what do you think of it?

JURGEN: What do we need broadcast quality for?

ESTHER: *(Picks up a piece of toast.)*

MOTHER: Hands off!

ESTHER: Mum!

MOTHER: Really. Well I'll turn the camera on and then you've all got to act as though I'm just coming downstairs.

FATHER: Read the instructions first *(Searches through the box for the instructions.)*

MOTHER: I can see that it works- Listen, I'll just turn the camera on and then you can sing happy birthday to me-

ESTHER: Again-

MOTHER: For the video.

FATHER: *(Has meantime found the instructions.)* Look Els-

MOTHER: I'm not an idiot Leo.

FATHER: It's an advanced piece of machinery-

MOTHER: It's on guys.

FATHER: *(Points to the camera.)* What d' you think they cost Jurgen.

JURGEN: *(Shrugs.)*

MOTHER: *(At the same time, looking through the camera.)* Start singing-

       FATHER and ESTHER start singing

JURGEN: *(Gets up.)*

MOTHER: Jurg-

JURGEN: I don't feel like it-

ESTHER: *(Continues singing.)*

FATHER: *(Gets up, follows JURGEN.)* Jurg, come on lad, just-

JURGEN: Why does everything always have to be so-

FATHER: Everything always, everything always-

JURGEN: Everything always yeah.

FATHER: *(Claps him on the shoulder.)* Hey Jurg-

JURGEN: *(Threateningly.)* Get your hands off me.

ESTHER: Hip hip-

FATHER: Hurrah- Jurg!

ESTHER: Hip hip-

MOTHER: It's suddenly gone all black.

ESTHER: Hurrah! Just film it mum!

MOTHER: I can't see a thing-

FATHER: Impossible.

ESTHER: *(Goes to pick up a piece of toast.)*

MOTHER: Hands off- Is this thing broken already.

FATHER: This thing, Els, it's a very expensive video camera.

MOTHER: So-

FATHER: So it can't be broken.

MOTHER: Has it got a guarantee Leo.

FATHER: It's bloody broadcast quality.

MOTHER: Whatever that is-

FATHER: Here, it's even says so in the instructions- *(To ESTHER.)* What does that say?

ESTHER: Broadcast quality.

FATHER: See?

MOTHER: But it doesn't work Leo.

FATHER: I'm not a complete idiot Els.

MOTHER: Leo-

FATHER: As if I got that thing out the Trade-It, as if I've turned up with some cut-price bargain or other. Here- *(Shows JURGEN the brandname on the video camera.)* What does that say? Right! Sony.

JURGEN: I think-

FATHER: Sony it says.

JURGEN: It's just the battery.

FATHER: *(As if he knew it all along.)* Exactly-

JURGEN: Or it's not the battery.

FATHER: Hang on-

MOTHER: A battery should last longer than five minutes-

JURGEN: Batteries run down, that's normal.

FATHER: That's common knowledge Els.

MOTHER: Well why don't they do something about it then?

FATHER: *(Wearily.)* If only life was that simple.

MOTHER: If something doesn't work you have to make it work.

FATHER: *(Suddenly very irritated.)* That's typical, that's so typical eh- Els, a battery is just, it's just-

JURGEN: You're supposed to charge it up first. *(Plugs the lead of the video camera into the electricity socket.)*

FATHER: I know that Jurgen.

MOTHER: Then you should have charged it up beforehand.

FATHER: It was still in the box!

MOTHER: Then you should have taken it out of the box!

FATHER: I can't just, I'm not going to-

MOTHER: You could have known that I'd want to film the whole brunch.

FATHER: But how was I supposed to-

MOTHER: *(Emphatically.)* This is my birthday Leo- Sorry guys, we're still sitting here because daddy was too stupid to charge up the video.

ESTHER: How long is that going to take then?

FATHER: Have a piece of toast to keep you going Esther.

ESTHER: *(Takes a piece of toast, relieved.)*

MOTHER: Put it back.

ESTHER: Mum-

MOTHER: Oh no Leo. It's not as simple as that. We're going to sit here quietly until that thing is charged up.

ESTHER: I'm almost falling to bits.

MOTHER: Talk to your father about that then dear.

ESTHER: Dad-

FATHER: *(Makes a helpless gesture, "I can't do anything about it".)*

ESTHER: Mum-

MOTHER: *(Motions to Father.)*

(Pause, everyone waits.)

JURGEN: *(Takes a piece of toast.)*

MOTHER: You just dare Jurgen-

JURGEN: *(Steers the piece of toast slowly towards his mouth.)*

MOTHER: I'm warning you Jurgen- You heard what I said- Leo-

FATHER: Come on Jurgen, let's just wait until the video-

MOTHER: *(Increasingly irate, furious, as Jurgen steers the piece of toast nearer and nearer to his mouth.)* You just dare Jurgen. You've been warned now. Just you dare boy. He's going to be sorry if he does Leo-

FATHER: *(Helplessly.)* Jurg, mate-

MOTHER: It'll be on your head. Oh, if you just dare. If you just-

JURGEN: *(Stuffs the whole piece of toast into his mouth in one go.)*

MOTHER: Okay Jurg. Okay.

JURGEN: *(Takes another piece of toast, and gives one to ESTHER too.)*

MOTHER: Fine. That's clear then.

ESTHER: *(Wants to eat the piece of toast, is in doubt.)*

MOTHER: *(Takes the piece of toast away.)* Right we'll just start all over again everyone.

ESTHER: Mum!

MOTHER: Not another word. I'm going to leave the room now and when I come back we're all going to try our best and make a nice day of it.

FATHER: Els.

MOTHER: We'll make a cosy, jolly and above all uncomplicated day of it.

JURGEN: Like this is uncomplicated.

MOTHER: Starting from now. *(Exits.)*

JURGEN: *(To ESTHER.)* Do you think we're deprived-

ESTHER: What do you mean?

JURGEN: With parents like this-

FATHER: *(Irritated.)* It's on guys- *(His mobile rings.)* Oh bloody hell! *(Looks at the display, answers the mobile.)* We're in the middle of the brunch. I haven't got time now, Esther and Jurgen are sitting at the table-

MOTHER: *(From outside in the hallway.)* Can I come in Leo?

FATHER: *(Shouts.)* Just a moment Els! *(Into the telephone.)* Listen, Els is coming in any minute, I'm sitting here with that new camera- (sees that the children don't understand who he's talking to.) I'll call you later- *(Irritated.)* I'm saying I'll call you later! *(Turns the phone off, shouts.)* Just one second Els- *(Holds the camera in front of his face.)* Okay guys-

JURGEN: Who was that?

FATHER: Someone from work.

JURGEN: How did he know we were having a brunch.

FATHER: Because I told him we were. *(Shouts.)* Okay Els!

JURGEN: What's it got to do with anyone from work?

FATHER: *(Takes the camera away from his face, irritated.)* I don't have to explain every little-

MOTHER: *(Has meanwhile entered, with a glass of champagne.)* Cheers everyone, to me!

FATHER: *(Quickly picks up the video camera again.)*

MOTHER: You've missed it now Leo.

FATHER: Just go back a second, just go back a second please.

MOTHER: Do you do this on purpose?

FATHER: I'm sorry. I just had to adjust something-

MOTHER: You just do it on purpose don't you! *(Exits.)*

FATHER: Els! Hey, for fucksake Els- *(Goes after her.)*

> *(Silence, JURGEN and ESTHER aren't sure what to do.)*

JURGEN: *(Sticks his finger up, listens.)*

ESTHER: What is it.

JURGEN: That silence, it's not normal. *(Pauses, listens.)* What are those two doing?

ESTHER: They'll be back in a minute.

> *(silence.)*

JURGEN: And who was he just talking to on the phone for instance.

ESTHER: Someone from his work.

JURGEN: That's not how you talk to someone from your work.

ESTHER: So what.

JURGEN: What's going on Es. They sit round the table night after night. Whispering away for hours.

ESTHER: I know.

JURGEN: Or he paces the floor and she stands dead still in front of the window. Night after night Es-

ESTHER: Der! I know.

JURGEN: That's not normal is it. Nobody sleeps here in this house. And during the day everyone acts as though nothing's going on.

ESTHER: Nothing is going on!

JURGEN: Rubbish. *(He grabs her arm.)* There are games being played here Esther.

ESTHER: Let go of my arm Jurg.

JURGEN: You know just as well as-

ESTHER: Let go. You're hurting me.

FATHER: *(Comes running in, quickly grabs the camera.)*

MOTHER: *(From the hallway.)* Yes?

FATHER: *(Calls.)* Okay!

MOTHER: *(Comes in again, with a glass of champagne.)* Cheers everyone, to me!

FATHER: To you, Els!

JURGEN: To you, Els!

ESTHER: Since when do you call her Els.

JURGEN: Since my mother became my best friend. *(To FATHER.)* Did you get that?

MOTHER: *(Meanwhile.)* God, what a brunch guys, I bent over backwards to do my best.

FATHER: It looks marvellous Els!

MOTHER: I should think it does, I bent over backwards- Are you nearly done Leo-

FATHER: Just let me decide for my-

MOTHER: I think if you came a little bit closer-

FATHER: *(Meanwhile walks forward, till he is stopped by the flex.)*

JURGEN: You can zoom-in as well-

FATHER: Can't you all behave as though you're not being filmed. *(Films Esther, who is sitting with her hands over her face.)* What's the matter darling?

ESTHER: I don't want to be in it.

MOTHER: But it's really nice Es, you can show it to your children later-

ESTHER: I don't want any children-

MOTHER: Why not darling-

ESTHER: I don't want to be a mother.

MOTHER: *(To FATHER.)* Where does she get it from eh. *(Kisses ESTHER, knowing that the camera is filming everything.)* Oh guys! I'm so proud of us, really I am. This is going to be a wonderful video. We're such a special family-

JURGEN: Fortunately we're not like auntie Thea-

MOTHER: *(Laughs.)* Really Jurg! Now I'll never be able to show Thea the video-

JURGEN: You should vary the angle a bit dad, otherwise it's boring.

FATHER: Jurg- *(Suddenly falls to his knees.)* It's supposed to be a bit of a spontaneous-

MOTHER: Can you still see the brunch at all like that Leo-

FATHER: Els-

MOTHER: *(Irritated.)* What now-

FATHER: Just behave as though you're not being filmed-

MOTHER: Well stop talking to me the whole time then.

FATHER: Okay okay.

JURGEN: *(Has meanwhile heaped a pile of smoked salmon onto his toast.)* Absolutely delicious Els-

MOTHER: *(Sees the pile of smoked salmon.)* Now Jurgen- *(To FATHER.)* Turn it off now Leo- Leo- Off-

FATHER: *(Turns the camera off.)*

JURGEN: We should employ a full-time cameraman actually. And then broadcast everything live. So the whole world can see how happy we are here. It is broadcast quality after all, do you like the idea- A sort of model family, you know, so people can learn from our example- *(Meanwhile JURGEN keeps piling on the smoked salmon calmly.)* What's the matter?

MOTHER: Are you going to behave normally or-

FATHER: *(Points to the smoked salmon.)* That was paid for with hard-earned money my lad-

MOTHER: That's not the point Leo-

FATHER: He thinks it all grows on trees.

MOTHER: Listen Leo-

FATHER: He thinks that everything round here is completely-

MOTHER: He doesn't think that at all-

JURGEN: I do-

FATHER: See.

MOTHER: Look at that smirk Leo-

JURGEN: I really never knew that it all cost money mum.

MOTHER: Look then. He's winding you up.

JURGEN: *(Piles half the smoked salmon on to **ESTHER**'s bread.)*

ESTHER: Jurgen!

JURGEN: *(Imitates her.)* Jurgen!

FATHER: Bloody hell Jurg!

ESTHER: He knows I don't like smoked salmon.

JURGEN: You probably think it grows on trees.

FATHER: I can see a big red mark. There, behind you on the wallpaper-

MOTHER: You're not going to let a kid like that take the mickey out-

FATHER: *(Furious.)* No-one here's going to take the mickey out of me.

JURGEN: Can't we ever just for once have a nice normal-

MOTHER: At least there are three of us who do want to have a nice time here. Leo! *(Motions to him to film her.)*

FATHER: *(Turns the camera on, films the part of the table where **MOTHER** and **ESTHER** are sitting.)*

FATHER: Fantastic Els!

ESTHER: (Calls out.) I don't want to be in it.

MOTHER: *(Piles her plate full with food, looking at the camera.)* You help yourself too Esther-

ESTHER: I'm not very hungry-

MOTHER: (Piles **ESTHER**'s plate full.) Just for the fun of it-

ESTHER: *(Crying.)* I'm just not very hungry.

MOTHER: What's wrong darling.

FATHER: You don't want to be in the video crying.

ESTHER: *(Still crying, hands over her face.)* I don't want to be in it at all.

JURGEN: *(Reassuringly.)* It's all right Es. It's not even on.

MOTHER: *(Fiercely.)* Shut up you.

FATHER: What do you mean?

JURGEN: If the little red light isn't on-

MOTHER: He's winding you up Leo.

FATHER: Hang on Els- What little red light Jurg-

MOTHER: Don't react to it.

FATHER: I've just been pressing in the on button.

JURGEN: Then it's already on and you're turning it off.

MOTHER: Leo!

FATHER: Just hang on. Jurg, mate-

JURGEN: You've been filming the very bits you didn't want to film. Now we've got a tape full of arguments in broadcast quality.

MOTHER: But I thought you'd read the instructions.

FATHER: Look, if you all know better-

MOTHER: You can read can't you Leo.

JURGEN: You can read can't you Leo.

FATHER: (Lays the camera down on the table.) Then someone else can do the filming.

MOTHER: That man is just too stupid for-

FATHER: Yeah but-

MOTHER: Well he is isn't he.

JURGEN: Quite right Els.

MOTHER: (Points to the table, which looks rather ravaged.) Now you've all touched everything you can't see how I bent over backwards anymore-

FATHER: I'll put the table straight again. (Starts putting the tabletop back in it's original state.)

MOTHER: That man is just unbelievable!

JURGEN: You should have married uncle Eric. Then this would never have happened.

FATHER: Jurg, mate-

MOTHER: You'll never put it right like that Leo.

FATHER: Look, just let me-

JURGEN: (Has meanwhile connected the video camera to the TV, we can see what he is filming. He shows **FATHER** the

camera.) Look dad. Can you see the little red light- That means it's on. *(Films FATHER, looks through the camera.)* What exactly are you doing?

FATHER: (Is meanwhile trying to put one of the dishes which had looked very attractive at first, for instance a potato salad, back into it's original state, using his bare hands.)

MOTHER: Turn that thing off Jurgen.

JURGEN: *(Points the camera at MOTHER.)* We zoom in on the world known as Els Beumer.

MOTHER: (Neatens her hair.) Jurg!

JURGEN: Each little mole, each pore, a genuine moustache even-

MOTHER: (Holds her hand in front of the camera lens.)

JURGEN: And all this in broadcast quality.

MOTHER: Jurg-

JURGEN: *(Points the camera at ESTHER.)* And the ugly little girl here, who's the spitting image of her mother-

ESTHER: I don't look like mummy!

JURGEN: What's so terrible about that? *(Films MOTHER.)*

MOTHER: Leave the child alone Jurgen.

JURGEN: Keep smiling Els- *(Points the camera at ESTHER.)* But Esther Beumer, do I understand that you're not too happy with such a jolly mother?

ESTHER: *(Holds her hands in front of her face.)* Don't Jurg.

JURGEN: Or if you see your father like this for instance, to take an example ... *(Films his father, who is still clumsily trying to put the table straight.)*

FATHER: What's that lad?

JURGEN: What comes up at that moment for example. *(Points the camera at ESTHER.)*

ESTHER: I don't know.

JURGEN: Come on Esther Beumer. He's a bit of an idiot isn't he? *(Points the camera at FATHER again.)*

FATHER: *(Stoically continues clearing up the table.)*

JURGEN: You were right you know Els. That man is too stupid for words. From the look of things.

ESTHER: It's not his fault Jurgen.

JURGEN: *(Points camera at **ESTHER** again.)* Is that so?

ESTHER: He's got to do it because of mummy.

MOTHER: What nonsense. That man is completely free!

JURGEN: *(Films **FATHER**.)* And what does Leo Beumer himself think about that?

MOTHER: Stop that Jurg.

JURGEN: When he's lying in bed at night, next to a snoring Els-

ESTHER: *(Can't help laughing.)*

MOTHER: I don't snore Jurg.

JURGEN: And he's thinking back over a day like to day for instance. Doesn't he maybe think he's just a little bit of a wimp then.

FATHER: Who are you talking about.

ESTHER: About Leo Beumer.

FATHER: I am Leo Beumer.

JURGEN: Could that be a coincidence.

ESTHER: *(Can't help laughing again.)*

JURGEN: We suddenly have Leo Beumer live in the broadcast-

ESTHER: *(Laughs.)*

FATHER: I don't understand what's so funny about-

JURGEN: But being Leo Beumer- What do you actually think about this. All this here. *(Films the room.)*

FATHER: What is there to think about it.

JURGEN: The whole situation. With you in it. This idiotic brunch which keeps having to start all over again. This ridiculous film which has to be made, at all cost.

FATHER: We're just trying to make the best of things here together.

MOTHER: Exactly!

JURGEN: I just think it's sad, how about you Es? *(Films **ESTHER**.)*

ESTHER: *(Can't help laughing again, loudly.)* Don't Jurgen.

JURGEN: *(Keeps filming **ESTHER**.)* That's the way it is. However much work that brunch took, however often we start all over again, it's just a crap birthday and it's going to stay one. Isn't it?

ESTHER: *(Laughs.)*

MOTHER: Turn that camera off.

JURGEN: You should keep laughing though. That ugly face is no good to anyone.

MOTHER: Turn that camera off Jurgen- Tell him to stop it Leo!

FATHER: Jurgen-

JURGEN: *(Films MOTHER.)* You wanted a video didn't you.

MOTHER: Not like this Jurgen-

JURGEN: But this is how we are Els-

MOTHER: Not at all.

JURGEN: This is our family.

MOTHER: Not true.

JURGEN: Don't be such a prat Els!

MOTHER: I'm your mother Jurg.

FATHER: She is your mother boy.

JURGEN: So what?

ESTHER: *(Can't help laughing again, loudly.)*

FATHER: I am your father eh.

JURGEN: *(To ESTHER.)* As if I didn't know.

FATHER: *(Confused.)* No but-

ESTHER: *(Laughs.)*

FATHER: And don't you forget it.

ESTHER: But you wouldn't forget it would you.

FATHER: No Esther-

ESTHER: *(Can't help laughing again.)*

FATHER: *(Amused by ESTHER's laughing.)* Now Es-

MOTHER: *(To JURGEN.)* You just like smashing things.

JURGEN: I'm only interested in the truth-

MOTHER: It all depends on how you see it.

JURGEN: I see a woman of forty-five with wrinkles, drooping breasts and a fat arse.

ESTHER: *(Can't help laughing again, loudly.)*

MOTHER: *(Astonished.)* That's not true.

JURGEN: I see what I see Els.

MOTHER: They think we're sisters. Esther-

ESTHER: *(Can't help laughing again, loudly.)*

FATHER: *(Laughs loudly with her.)*

MOTHER: Say something Leo.

FATHER: *(Through his laughter.)* Eh guys – Guys-

> *(Everyone laughs even louder.)*

MOTHER: Leo! *(Bursts into tears, like a little girl.)*

ESTHER: *(Shocked, stops laughing abruptly.)*

FATHER: *(Placatingly.)* Els!

MOTHER: *(To FATHER.)* I can't just, it isn't just-

JURGEN: *(Filming her.)* This will look great Els!

MOTHER: *(She tries to hit Jurgen weakly, exits.)*

> *(Silence.)*

FATHER: *(Looks at ESTHER and JURGEN, doesn't really know what to say, tries a little laugh, looks at his watch, loosens his bow-tie a bit more.)*

JURGEN: *(Picks up a piece of toast, starts to eat.)*

ESTHER: *(Also takes a piece of toast.)*

> Suddenly **MOTHER** starts to cry very loudly in the kitchen; when that's been going on a while **FATHER** straightens his bow-tie, smiles at the children and goes towards the kitchen

JURGEN: And what if you didn't go-

FATHER: *(Turns.)* Eh-

JURGEN: You heard me.

FATHER: Jurg. Mate-

JURGEN: No-ones says you've got to go to the kitchen.

FATHER: Just wait a few years till you're-

JURGEN: I wouldn't go to the kitchen then either.

FATHER: You can't know that-

JURGEN: I'd just stay sitting here.

FATHER: Yes but-

JURGEN: D'you want to bet I'd do that. *(Offers FATHER a piece of toast.)* Here- Come on dad-

FATHER: *(Sits down.)* I don't know guys- *(He goes to take a bite of his toast, at that moment MOTHER begins to cry even harder in the kitchen.)*

ESTHER: Dad-

FATHER: *(Gets up.)*

JURGEN: If you go now you can forget it.

ESTHER: Don't be so ridiculous-

FATHER: Listen now lad-

ESTHER: You've got to go now dad-

FATHER: I'll be right back-

JURGEN: You heard what I said eh-

FATHER: Then we'll carry on talking immediately-

JURGEN: I think not.

FATHER: Okay Jurg? *(Exits, MOTHER immediately stops crying.)*

> *(Silence.)*

JURGEN: *(Points at ESTHER.)*

ESTHER: What?

JURGEN: If you're not with me, you're against me Es- I was listening carefully just now-

ESTHER: *(Can't help laughing.)*

JURGEN: You're going to have to make a choice too-

ESTHER: Oh give over-

JURGEN: You'll see- *(Takes a piece of toast, eats, pause, keeps looking at her.)*

ESTHER: What?

JURGEN: Why did he need to go to the kitchen just now.

ESTHER: Otherwise she'd never stop crying.

JURGEN: How do you know that for certain.

ESTHER: You know as well as I do.

JURGEN: We're going round in circles Es. If everyone round here keeps on doing what they always do then it's just going to go on and on and on and on-

ESTHER:	JURGEN:
I don't understand you Jurgen	*(At the same time.)* I don't understand you Jurgen.

ESTHER:	JURGEN:
Just stop it!	Just stop it!

JURGEN: See-

ESTHER:	JURGEN:
Don't be so ridiculous.	Don't be so ridiculous.

JURGEN: See I know exactly how it goes round here.

ESTHER:	JURGEN:
I don't understand-	I don't understand- Of course you don't understand.

    (Silence.)

ESTHER: What are we going to do then Jurg.

JURGEN: We've got to stop them Es. If we don't do it nobody will.

FATHER: *(Whispers.)* Everything's fine- *(Comes in, steering MOTHER before him. MOTHER has black rings around her eyes from running mascara, her hair is awry, she stares ahead blankly, allows herself to be lead to her chair by FATHER.)*

    Right, well-

JURGEN: *(Starts reading his book again.)*

FATHER: You too Jurg, just listen-

JURGEN: *(Reads on calmly.)*

FATHER: I've just had a little talk with your er mother-

ESTHER: Why are you whispering like that-

FATHER: *(Whispers.)* Ssht, hang on Es. Jurg. I mean. So I've just had a little talk with er mummy, eh Els. Everything's fine. Sit yourself down Els *(Pushes MOTHER down in her chair).* But we think it would be better, are you listening Jurg, we think it would be better if we just started all over again.

ESTHER: Don't be so ridiculous dad.

FATHER: *(Emphatically.)* I'm not being ridiculous. We'll start all over again one more time, with a clean slate- We'll make a cosy, jolly and above all uncomplicated day of it, eh Els- That might seem a little odd-

JURGEN: Odd no-

FATHER: No eh- *(To MOTHER.)* See they do understand Els-

JURGEN: I understand exactly what you mean.

FATHER: Understand Esther. We're just going to all try- We're all going to make the best of it, I mean, a cosy er uncomplicated er- Understand Els. I mean er- *(To ESTHER.)* Perhaps you can er the video- *(Gives her the video camera.)*

ESTHER: *(Stands up hesitantly, takes the camera.)*

FATHER: Jolly good. *(Stands up, with raised glass.)* Cheers guys. To mummy. Jurg. Es!

ESTHER: Cheers mummy!

MOTHER: *(Raises her glass, blankly.)*

ESTHER: *(Hesitantly.)* Mummy-

FATHER: Marvellous brunch Els! *(Butters a piece of bread, heartily.)*

MOTHER: *(Stuffs a sandwich in her mouth in one go, with full mouth.)* Do you find me attractive Leo?

FATHER: *(Chokes on his bread, splutters.)*

What kind of a question is that.

MOTHER: I just want to know if you still find me attractive.

FATHER: Just because Jurgen-

JURGEN: I didn't say anything!

MOTHER: *(Snaps at JURGEN.)* Shut up you!

ESTHER: Shall I film this as well?

MOTHER: *(Emphatically.)* I'm forty-five Leo.

FATHER: I'm not going to discuss this in front of the children-

MOTHER: Why not? They're used to it.

FATHER: *(Trying to sound convincing.)* I still find you very attractive Els.

JURGEN: This is unbelievable-

FATHER: Keep out of it Jurg.

MOTHER: But Leo-

FATHER: *(To MOTHER, wearily.)* Shall we just drop it.

JURGEN: I'm not doing anything!

FATHER: *(Aggressively.)* Shall we just drop it Jurg- *(To MOTHER.)* Just look how marvellous this brunch-

MOTHER: *(Stands up, grabs FATHER by the lapels of his jacket, emphatically.)* I'm alive Leo.

FATHER: *(Anxiously.)* For god's sake Els!

MOTHER: Can you feel it. I'm doing this Leo *(Shakes him back and forth.)* Can you feel it?

FATHER: Hang on Els-

MOTHER: *(Releases him, slaps him round the face.)*

ESTHER: *(Can't help laughing loudly again.)*

MOTHER: Just stop that stupid laughing-

ESTHER: *(Tries her best not to laugh.)* I can't help it!

FATHER: *(Feels the place where she slapped him.)* I-

ESTHER: *(Can't help laughing really loudly again.)*

MOTHER: Esther!

ESTHER: *(Laughing.)* I can't stop it.

FATHER: *(Feels his nose, there's blood on his hand, he shows it to MOTHER.)* My god-

MOTHER: *(Parrots him.)* My God- Are you a man or a mouse Leo- Is this a man or a mouse guys!

ESTHER: *(Can't help laughing loudly again, Jurgen laughs with her.)*

MOTHER: *(Laughs loudly with the children.)* For godsake! I need a breath of fresh air. And some space around me- *(Exits.)*

FATHER: *(Remains sitting.)*

> *ESTHER* and *JURGEN* are having hysterics.

FATHER: This is, this isn't- *(His mobile phone rings, he turns it on, aggressively.)*

Why do you keep ringing me- *(He walks quickly out of the door.)*

JURGEN: *(Stops laughing abruptly, points towards the door that FATHER has disappeared through, silence.)*

ESTHER: (Looks at him, bursts out laughing again.)

JURGEN: I'd stop if I were you-

ESTHER: *(Through her laughter.)* I can't stop-

JURGEN: *(Slaps her round the face.)*

ESTHER: *(Laughing.)* Not helping-

JURGEN: *(Slaps harder.)*

ESTHER: Harder-

JURGEN: *(Slaps her harder.)*

ESTHER: *(Stops laughing, says calmly.)* Ow.

JURGEN: *(Goes to slap her again.)*

ESTHER: *(Deflects him.)* It's already stopped.

JURGEN: *(With hand raised.)* Are you sure?

ESTHER: Thanks.

JURGEN: *(Smashes a plate.)* Don't mention it.

ESTHER: *(Laughing.)* Jurg!

JURGEN: That's the power Es. Because I wanted to hit you, then the power's already in my arm. It has to get out some other way. *(Smashes another plate.)* I'm full of it, with that power- *(Takes **MOTHER** and **FATHER**'s plates, shuts his eyes.)* It bubbles up from deep down inside. And then suddenly- *(Goes to smash the plates together.)*

ESTHER: Jurg!

JURGEN: *(Moves the plates as if they are magnetic.)* Can you see how much they want to smash themselves to pieces, I'm just helping them a bit. *(Smashes the two plates together, looks at the shards.)* Everything's breaking up around here. Have you noticed that too. Even the plants are on their last legs. Do you know why that is Es-

ESTHER: I don't know.

JURGEN: We're living with two vampires. They won't be happy until everything around them is as dead as they are. Here- *(Presses his hands to her face.)*

ESTHER: *(Shudders.)*

JURGEN: Can you feel it. *(He takes her hands.)* Your hands are exactly the same. We've got to get out of here Es. We'll end up stone cold if we don't watch out.

ESTHER: *(Pulls her hands away, walks over to the cupboard and takes out a big pile of plates.)*

Jurgen!

JURGEN: See. You've got the power in you too.

ESTHER: *(Hesitates.)* What shall I do Jurg?

JURGEN: It's just a question of letting go. Eyes closed. Can you feel it.

ESTHER: *(Raises the plates, closes her eyes, hesitates.)* They'll be back soon-

JURGEN: So what-

ESTHER: I don't know anyone who does this.

JURGEN: Because it's not like this anywhere else.

ESTHER: *(Hesitantly.)* I don't know Jurg- *(Puts the plates on the table.)*

JURGEN: Fine. You're on your own from now on then. *(Walks away.)*

ESTHER: What are you going to do?

JURGEN: I'm leaving. *(Exits, walks past FATHER, who is just coming in.)*

FATHER: *(Takes Jurgen by the arm.)*

JURGEN: *(Pushes Father away.)*

FATHER: Jurg. Calm down. Look, man to man-

JURGEN: *(Surprised.)* Eh?

FATHER: Man to man eh- *(Spreads his hands, gesture of reconciliation.)* Hey-

JURGEN: *(Smiles, exits.)*

> *(Pause.)*

FATHER: *(Sits down at the table, without noticing that **ESTHER** is in the room, takes out his mobile phone, looks at the door, quickly taps in a number, goes and stands by the window, speaks quickly, whispering.)* It's me. I'm still at home, no, just listen, on my own yes, in the dining room, no, the brunch still hasn't got going- Els is worse than ever, completely flipped her lid. *(Controlled anger.)* As soon as I can! I can't just leave like this, with things this way- I can't leave her alone with the children like this- *(Wearily.)* Just be a bit more patient- I know that, but just be a little bit more- *(Pretends he's heard something.)* Oh gosh, I think there's someone coming, I've got to hang up. Yeah, me too, but I've really got to- *(Presses the off button, takes out his handkerchief, dabs his nose, feels something pressing on his Adam's apple, coughs, feels, finds the bowtie, loosens it, suddenly starts to weep, after a while a glass suddenly falls off the table without warning.)*

ESTHER: *(Startled.)* Whaa!

FATHER: *(Also startled.)* Christ, Esther, I nearly jumped out of my skin- *(Tries to conceal the fact that he's been crying, quickly wipes his eyes, points to the glass.)* How long have you been standing there?

ESTHER: You said I had to film everything-

FATHER: Oh darling, you don't have to film this- *(Goes to take the camera, ESTHER takes a step backwards.)*

ESTHER: Why were you crying just now?

FATHER: Was I crying just now?

ESTHER: Don't you think it's nice here any more?

FATHER: I think it's extremely nice here. We're going to have our cosy brunch in a minute- You just see. When mummy and Jurgen come downstairs-

ESTHER: Jurgen says you two stay up every night-

FATHER: Jurgen's just making it up-

ESTHER: He says you're both ghosts-

FATHER: *(Over-jolly.)* What nonsense!

ESTHER: Jurgen says-

FATHER: *(Suddenly aggressive.)* That boy's just got to shut his- you've all just got to- it's just got to be a bit more- *(Sees that ESTHER is scared, tries to put it right.)* Now listen darling. There's nothing wrong. We've just got to take no notice of Jurgen at all, he's going through a phase er what d'you call it a sort of phase- Hey, Es- *(Opens his arms.)*

ESTHER: *(Scared.)*

FATHER: Just come over here. *(Pause.)* Es-

ESTHER: No-

FATHER: What is it darling?

ESTHER: You look so weird.

FATHER: *(Feels his bow-tie.)* I don't look weird at all-

ESTHER: You do-

FATHER: *(Can't control himself, rips his bow-tie off.)* Better? Isn't it? *(Sweetly.)* Hey poppet- *(Impatiently.)* Look what the bloody hell's-

ESTHER: You're acting weird.

FATHER: *(Helplessly.)* I- *(Rubs his head.)*

ESTHER: You look weird and you sound weird.

FATHER: *(Aggressively.)* Look you've just got to-

ESTHER: Who was that on the telephone just now.

FATHER: You mustn't get so wound up- *(Gets up, walks towards **ESTHER**, tries to sound unconcerned.)* Come on now darling-

ESTHER: *(Picks up a plate.)* Don't come any closer-

FATHER: *(At a loss what to do, let's his arm flop to his sides.)* Look what's the matter?

ESTHER: It's just as if you're not you-

FATHER: But I am me Es- *(Opens arms.)* Look. Can you see I'm me. You can see that I'm-

ESTHER: It's just like someone else is saying that-

FATHER: Saying what.

ESTHER: That.

FATHER: I'm saying that myself- Here. I'm saying this. This. You see. I'm just, just myself, I- *(Walks towards her, goes to take hold of her.)*

ESTHER: *(Smashes the plate, takes a new plate from the table.)*

FATHER: *(Walks towards her resolutely, grabs hold of her, tries to take the plate away from her, **ESTHER** tries to struggle free, **FATHER** holds her tight.)* Don't be so ridiculous!

MOTHER: *(Comes in, sees **FATHER** and **ESTHER**.)*

ESTHER: *(Tries to struggle free.)*

FATHER: *(Tries to kiss her on the head.)* Hush now poppet, please-

MOTHER: *(Calmly.)* Let go of that child Leo.

FATHER: *(Scared, lets go of **ESTHER**.)*

ESTHER: He wants me to go to him the whole time but I don't want to- He wants me to-

MOTHER: At a given moment when little girls get older a certain tension arises between them and their father, that's very normal. And if daddy can't deal with that in a grown-up way then you'll just have to grow up a bit.

FATHER: You don't really bloody think I'm-

MOTHER: *(Hits **FATHER**.)* See. The only thing that helps. Learned something have you.

FATHER: *(Hits **MOTHER** back.)*

ESTHER: *(Smashes another plate.)*

MOTHER: Esther!

FATHER: *(Resolutely.)* Are we going to behave normally round here again?

ESTHER: *(Smashes another plate.)*

FATHER: I mean it you know!

MOTHER: Go and fetch Jurgen. He's locked himself in his room-

FATHER: Hang on a minute-

MOTHER: I won't let anything else ruin my birthday. Go and fetch that boy Leo.

FATHER: But what shall I- what am I supposed to-

MOTHER: Be a man Leo. Get it over with. *(Puts **ESTHER** in her place at table.)*

FATHER: *(Doesn't know what to do.)*

Some plaster dust falls from the ceiling.

FATHER: *(Exits.)*

ESTHER: *(Stares in blank bewilderment.)*

MOTHER: You think you're going through something eh-

ESTHER: *(Confused.)* I don't know.

MOTHER: This is just the beginning. It's only going to get worse.

ESTHER: *(Starts to cry.)*

MOTHER: Don't start bawling Es. If anyone's unhappy round here it's me. You've still got your life ahead of you. Look at me.

ESTHER: *(Looks at her **MOTHER**.)*

MOTHER: I was just like you, when I met him, almost exactly like you. *(Points to the door through which **FATHER** has just exited.)* That man, that man has completely broken me. In fifteen years he's made an old woman out of me. And do you know why that is. Because I was too weak.

ESTHER: *(Turns her face away.)* I'd rather not-

MOTHER: Rather not my foot. This is life Esther, get used to it. Before you know it you'll be just like me. You watch.

ESTHER: You're lying! *(Cries, looking at the floor so that **MOTHER** won't see her crying.)*

MOTHER: You're crying now aren't you.

ESTHER: *(Keeps looking at the ground.)*

MOTHER: *(Takes her by the chin, forces her to look at her.)* Do you think I haven't cried. Of course I've cried. I've cried myself ugly. Wrinkles on my face, grey hairs- my whole body cried flaccid. Here. This is what it's done for me. *(Pinches her belly.)* Old flesh. Here. *(Takes **ESTHER**'s hand.)*

ESTHER: *(Pulls her hand away.)*

MOTHER: Stop that bloody crying! That's exactly what they want you to do - cry yourself flaccid so you can't excite them any more. *(Grabs **ESTHER**'s hands.)*

ESTHER: *(Tries to struggle free.)*

MOTHER: *(Holds on tightly.)* Ssshh. Listen. *(Squeezes **ESTHER**'s wrists hard.)*

ESTHER: *(Softly.)* Ow!

MOTHER: You've got to harden up girlie. Soft outside, but hard as stone inside. Let them stub out a burning cigarette-end on your arm. *(Squeezes **ESTHER**'s wrists tighter.)*

ESTHER: Ow!

MOTHER: Let them provoke the blood from under your fingernails. And keep a friendly smile on your face. Radiant. Keep smiling your most seductive smile. *(Emphatically.)* As long as you stay beautiful you'll be the boss girlie. *(Lets go of **ESTHER**.)* Here. *(Gives her a handkerchief.)* Dry those tears, before they burn through to your insides.

ESTHER: *(Dries her tears.)*

MOTHER: Breathe.

ESTHER: *(Takes a deep breath, looks at **MOTHER**, outraged.)*

MOTHER: Let the blood stream through you. It keeps you young.

ESTHER: *(Nods: yes.)*

MOTHER: And now smile-

ESTHER: *(Conjures a little smile on her face, that looks dangerous.)*

MOTHER: That's right kid.

ESTHER: *(With **MOTHER**'s voice.)* That's right kid.

> Suddenly **FATHER**'s mobile phone rings, which he's left lying on the table

ESTHER: *(Jumps, leaps up, goes and stands a little distance away from the table.)*

MOTHER: *(Looks at the display, turns the telephone off.)* What is it. You're not scared of a telephone are you. *(Exits.)*

ESTHER: *(Sits down. It is quiet, she doesn't know what to do, sees the pile of plates on the table, goes over to the table and drops them.)*

JURGEN: *(Comes in, sees the shards.)* See, you can do it!

ESTHER: Someone just phoned again.

JURGEN: Who was it.

ESTHER: I don't know. Leo Beumer just phoned again too.

JURGEN: Phoned who.

ESTHER: He wouldn't tell me.

JURGEN: What was he saying?

ESTHER: I filmed it. *(Gives him the camera.)*

JURGEN: *(He rewinds the camera, watches the scene in which FATHER telephones, then grabs FATHER's mobile from the table, presses a button, listens, looks shocked, hangs up quickly.)*

ESTHER: Who was it-

JURGEN: Who do you think.

ESTHER: I don't know.

JURGEN: *(Dials the number again, puts his handkerchief over the mouthpiece, talks fast and business-like.)* It's me, I've got to talk quietly, listen, they're going out soon, Els is completely hysterical, she's going to the beach with the kids. Come and get me in a little while. I've arranged everything. I've got to hang up now. *(Hangs up, a bit more plaster dust falls from the ceiling.)* We're leaving Es. Before the whole thing comes down on our heads.

Exit ESTHER and JURGEN, a little later the ceiling lamp falls down, with a great crash, FATHER and MOTHER come running in, MOTHER with dustpan and brush, immediately sweeps up the bits.

MOTHER: I told you you should have used a rawl-plug when you put that lamp up.

FATHER: I did use one Els. I just don't understand why- (Sees his telephone lying on the table, quickly picks it up.)

MOTHER: Everything you put together falls apart just as fast. *(Meanwhile sees FATHER picking up the phone.)* Do you honestly think you have to be reachable all the time.

FATHER: I've already turned it off.

MOTHER: Who's going to phone you today anyway Leo.

FATHER: I said I'd turned it off.

(Pause, MOTHER keeps looking at FATHER.)

MOTHER: Why don't you want to talk Leo.

FATHER: What do you want to talk about the whole time.

MOTHER: There's something going on, I can feel it.

FATHER: I just want a nice day, to make a nice day of it together. *(Gets up.)* I'm going to fetch Jurgen.

MOTHER: Why are you so keen to leave.

FATHER: What do you mean?

MOTHER: You want to leave now Leo don't you.

FATHER: You mean now, I mean er, what do you mean?

MOTHER: You mustn't keep asking counter-questions.

FATHER: What the hell are you driving at Els?

MOTHER: You're doing it again now Leo! We're going to talk till we've got to the bottom of this. *(Meanwhile, takes FATHER's hands, lets go of them again quickly.)* Jesus. Leo. You're ice cold.

FATHER: I'm just a bit hungry.

MOTHER: *(Feels his forehead.)* Leo!

ESTHER and JURGEN comes downstairs, they both have a rucksack on their back and are wearing travel clothes. The light changes so that we only see JURGEN and ESTHER.

JURGEN: Sometimes it all just gets too much. Then you're full up inside, too many impressions, too much energy. Then there's no room for anything else, you can only close yourself off, so that nothing else gets in. That happened the day I went away. Packed my rucksack and left the house by the back door together with my sister. It was derelict, the house we lived in. The plaster was falling off the walls, you had to keep knocking the dust out of your hair. At night the snow used to drift straight through the walls, it was that icy. Then you might as well sleep outside, under a bridge, at the homeless shelter or on a bench in the park in the summer. I bought a packet of cigarettes, it was high time to take up smoking. If you've been walking round the whole day then you need a bit of comfort. A cup of coffee. A cigarette. A glass of beer of an evening. Those are the things that start to count. And in time a woman. Not a girlfriend to live together with. A woman for now and then. No family for us. We weren't much good at that, my sister and I.

ESTHER: I thought it was so chilly in Holland. It was almost always miserable. Your coat all wet, your hair plastered to your head, a trickle of water down your neck, shivering, I was actually shivering the whole time in Holland. That's why we went to France, my brother and I. If you keep walking you just end up there. Always in a southerly direction, every day a bit further and suddenly you see the Mediterranean in the distance. Vegetables and fruit, it just grows at the roadside. You wash in the sea, spend the whole day on the beach. After a week or two you're brown. I let my hair grow, Jurgen stopped shaving and nobody recognised us any more. There are empty farms all over the place there, we've seen them so often on holiday. You just put a new roof on, borrow tools from a farmer. The houses don't belong to anyone. No-one's interested in a ghost-house like that, they don't dare go there, at night. They're happy to see a light burning inside again. And it means new customers for them as well, you mustn't forget that.

Light changes back.

FATHER: What's this all about.

ESTHER: I'm not allowed to say anything. *(Goes to walk on.)*

MOTHER: *(Goes and stands in front of the door.)* Not on your life. Leo!

FATHER: *(Holds JURGEN back.)*

JURGEN: *(Threateningly.)* Don't touch me.

MOTHER: *(To ESTHER.)* What are you two up to.

ESTHER: I'm not allowed to say anything-

MOTHER: *(Goes to take ESTHER's rucksack off, ESTHER resists but MOTHER finally gets hold of the rucksack, empties it out, a pile of photo albums falls out.)* What do you want with all these photo albums-

ESTHER: I'm not allowed to say anything.

JURGEN: *(Starts repacking the rucksack.)*

FATHER: Leave that!

MOTHER: *(Has meanwhile pulled out an envelope from the bank from amongst all the stuff, pulls out a wad of banknotes from it, in amazement, to FATHER.)* They've got a couple of thousand euros on them-

FATHER: *(Looks at the envelope.)* Where did you get that from?

JURGEN: Where d'you think- *(Snatches envelope back from MOTHER.)*

MOTHER: *(Threateningly.)* Jurg!

JURGEN: A friend's been saving it for us *(He continues repacking ESTHER's rucksack.)*

MOTHER: What kind of a friend?

JURGEN: A sort of sponsor.

MOTHER: And what's this friend called then Jurgen?

JURGEN: He'd rather remain anonymous I think.

MOTHER: *(To FATHER.)* What the hell are they up to Leo!

FATHER: *(Tries to take the money away from JURGEN.)*

JURGEN: *(Resists FATHER.)* Don't touch me-

FATHER: *(Pushes JURGEN backwards.)*

JURGEN: *(Pushes his FATHER backwards, FATHER falls over.)*

MOTHER: Are you completely mad- *(Grabs JURGEN by the arm.)*

JURGEN: *(Pulls himself free.)*

ESTHER: *(Breaks a glass from the table, holds it threateningly towards MOTHER.)* Leave him alone- *(Nicks MOTHER's arm with the glass.)*

MOTHER: Ow! Esther! *(Shows her arm to FATHER.)* Leo!

FATHER: *(Grabs ESTHER by the arm.)*

ESTHER: *(Drops the glass.)*

JURGEN: *(Grabs **FATHER** by the arm.)*

FATHER: *(Throws **JURGEN** to the floor.)*

ESTHER: *(Breaks another glass.)*

MOTHER: Bloody hell. Esther!

JURGEN: *(Tries to get up.)*

FATHER: *(Pushes him back to the floor.)* You think you're tough don't you eh. *(Gives him a kick in his side.)*

ESTHER: *(Stands with the glass in her hand, doesn't know what to do.)*

JURGEN: *(Tries to get up again.)*

FATHER: *(Pushes him back to the floor again.)* You thought you could take me on.

ESTHER: *(Pulls the tablecloth and the whole brunch from the table in one go.)*

MOTHER: Are you completely mad. *(Goes to hit her.)*

ESTHER: *(Avoids the blow.)*

FATHER: *(Meanwhile to **JURGEN**.)* I'm the boss round here, all right.

JURGEN: *(Tries to get up again.)*

FATHER: *(Kicks him in the side again, **JURGEN** groans.)*

ESTHER: *(Throws herself on **FATHER**, hangs on his back, her arms round his neck.)*

FATHER: *(To **JURGEN**.)* Don't put it on. I know exactly what I'm doing *(Points to the place where he just kicked **JURGEN**.)* There's nothing there- *(Kicks him again.)*

ESTHER: Stop it! *(While still hanging on his back, she has a vegetable knife in her hand.)*

FATHER: *(Kicks him again.)* There are no vital organs there at all.

MOTHER: That child's got a knife Leo!

FATHER: *(Throws **ESTHER** off his back, grabs **JURGEN**'s head.)* You didn't want to talk to me like a man did you eh.

JURGEN: *(With muffled voice.)* Arsehole.

FATHER: Because you don't know how to. *(Taps **JURGEN**'s head with his shoe.)* Have you ever had a woman Jurg?

JURGEN: None of your business.

FATHER: You haven't got a clue. I can smell it. The only things you know are out of books. As long as you haven't had a woman laddie, I'm the boss around here. *(Takes the money from **JURGEN**, stuffs the envelope in his jacket.)*

ESTHER: *(Furious.)* You can't just put our money in your pocket.

MOTHER: As long as we don't know where that money came from it's ours.

JURGEN: *(Angry, almost in tears.)* That money is his! I took it from his desk. That money is his!

FATHER: *(Panting.)* So what Jurg. So what?

MOTHER: What are you doing with so much money!

FATHER: What do you mean?

MOTHER: What were you planning on doing with it!

FATHER: *(Panting.)* This here- *(Pulls the envelope out of his inside pocket.)* is an envelope full of freedom Els.

MOTHER: Don't be so ridiculous.

FATHER: Well spotted lad. You can use this to escape.

MOTHER: Leo-

FATHER: Listen Els. I'm going away. I can't stand it here any longer. You've got to understand. I didn't want it like this- I was looking forward to a nice brunch. I wanted us to be able to look back on a pleasant afternoon, the last afternoon that I'd live in this house with you-

MOTHER: You were going to leave me on my birthday-

FATHER: *(Angrily.)* It was a farewell Els. For me this was a farewell!

MOTHER: *(Exits.)*

FATHER: Listen guys. I've got to get out. I can't be myself here any more. Do you know what I mean. I'm continually criticised round here. By you as well. And rightly too. Perfectly rightly. He's a weak twerp, the Leo Beumer that you know. It's perfectly understandable he's not allowed to come with to parent's evenings. That nobody ever laughs at his corny little jokes. That he looks dreadful in shorts. That he buys a ridiculous pair of sunglasses every year. But you don't know who he really is, Leo Beumer. Like when your mother used to sit on the back of my bike, with her arms round me tight, after school parties. Riding through the polder, with the sun coming up. Like when we all used to go camping. France, Spain, Greece. The way we could put the tent up together. When you sometimes saw other families bungling it. We had the whole thing sorted out in next to no time. And it was a very complicated bungalow tent too eh. But everyone knew exactly what they were doing. I was so proud of you kids. And you were just as proud of me. "That's my father", you used to go round the whole camp site like that Jurgen. Telling everyone you met. "That man is my father". I used to chuck you onto the lilo in the sea from the beach, just like that. Four or five metres I'd fling you through the air. And you'd be shouting your heads off. That was Leo Beumer guys. Behind the barbeque, the amusing banter, you could have a laugh with that man, your mother as well. We did some laughing in the beginning. In the middle of the night. So loud the neighbours would start thumping on the floor. Oh god, we always had friends round then. Always a crate of beer on the balcony, bottles of rosé in the fridge. Do you know what I mean guys. It was never the intention to end up here- like this, I mean- I'm not Leo Beumer. I mean, the real Leo Beumer who's in here- *(Thumps his chest.)* somewhere, deep inside. I can feel him in there, very far away. I can never become who I was again here. I've turned grey here. Dusty. Do you understand that I've got to go. That I saved up in order to go. Do you understand that that's better for everyone. Do you understand that guys. I mean. I even saved you Esther, you nearly suffocated in the hood of your sleeping bag, but I was just in time remember- You do remember Es don't you. Es-

MOTHER enters with a suitcase, she is wearing a raincoat and walks towards the door.

MOTHER: Listen children. Mummy's going away for a while. You mustn't be upset. It's nothing to do with you. Mummy hasn't been getting on very well with daddy recently-

FATHER: They're not toddlers any more Els.

MOTHER: Because daddy is having a relationship with auntie Thea.

FATHER: Els!

MOTHER: I'm not mad Leo. Daddy is having a relationship with auntie Thea and he doesn't want to talk about it and that's made mummy a bit tired and she needs to go away for a rest.

FATHER: Listen guys-

MOTHER: Somewhere in the woods, with lots of other mothers who are just as tired as mummy. And when I come back again we'll throw a big party with balloons and lemonade-

FATHER: Why do you always have to make everything so complicated Els.

MOTHER: O god, nemonade, do you remember Jurg, that's what you used to say, can I have a glass of nemonade, nemonade, oh god *(Starts crying.)* I've really got to go now-

FATHER: You're not going to leave the children alone are you.

MOTHER: Then you take them with you Leo. You just call auntie Thea mummy from now on, nothing else changes. Bye darlings- *(Walks off.)*

(Doorbell rings, MOTHER jumps.)

MOTHER: Jesus, who could that be. I look awful. *(Tidies her hair.)* It's a mess. *(Brushes some broken crockery to one side.)* Give me a hand will you-

ESTHER: *(Has meanwhile walked to the intercom.)* Hello?

VOICE OF AUNTIE THEA: Hello?

ESTHER: Hello?

VOICE OF AUNTIE THEA: Esther! Haven't you gone to the beach?

MOTHER: *(Walks to the intercom.)* Thea! I thought you couldn't come today.

VOICE OF AUNTIE THEA: Leo said you'd all gone to the beach. Is Leo there?

FATHER: *(At the same time, overly brightly, towards the intercom.)* Hello Thea. Great! *(Trying to make it clear to her that she's come at the wrong moment.)* We're right in the middle of the birthday Thea, just come in-

VOICE OF AUNTIE THEA: *(Confused.)* You said I could come and fetch you, you said-

MOTHER: Unbelievable Leo.

FATHER: *(Walks to the intercom.)* Thea, listen Thea-

VOICE OF AUNTIE THEA: Christ Leo, how embarrassing!

MOTHER: Doesn't matter Thea. He is coming, he's on his way.

VOICE OF AUNTIE THEA: Listen Els, let me in, let's just talk.

MOTHER: Look just take him, it's no problem at all, we've had enough of him anyway haven't we guys.

VOICE OF AUNTIE THEA: He came to me of his own accord. I didn't lift a finger Els! Honestly-

MOTHER: It's no problem. You can take him. Or I'll go and you can move in here, that's all right too. I got my bag packed, you just say the word-

ESTHER: I don't want auntie Thea to come and live here.

MOTHER: Did you hear that Thea, so that's out then. Come on Leo, you're holding her up.

ESTHER: I don't want daddy to go away.

VOICE OF AUNTIE THEA: Perhaps it's better if I leave-

FATHER: I'll phone you later.

MOTHER: *(At the same time as Father.)* You stay there Thea.

FATHER: *(Completely confused.)* Els-

VOICE OF AUNTIE THEA: I'll wait one more minute Leo!

ESTHER: I don't want you to go daddy!

MOTHER: You can't have it all ways Esther.

ESTHER: *(Turns the key of the security shutter system, it slowly grows dark in the room.)* I don't want him to go.

JURGEN: Don't do that Es!

ESTHER: *(In the intercom.)* Go away Thea!

VOICE OF AUNTIE THEA: There's a shutter thing coming down out here, a sort of-

FATHER: This is the final bloody straw!

JURGEN: Just go then will you!

FATHER: The final straw this is!

VOICE OF AUNTIE THEA: Leo?

JURGEN: *(Has meanwhile fetched **FATHER**'s coat from the coat-hook.)* Here. Come on.

ESTHER: Jurg!

(The security shutters are down.)

ESTHER: *(Takes the key out of the security shutter system.)*

JURGEN: *(Furious.)* Give me that key.

ESTHER: You said you'd help me Jurgen.

VOICE OF AUNTIE THEA: Leo!

FATHER: I can't leave like this Thea!

JURGEN: *(Shouts.)* He's on his way!

FATHER: Mind your own business.

VOICE OF AUNTIE THEA: Half a minute to go Leo.

FATHER: Fucking hell!

JURGEN: Are you a man or a mouse.

FATHER: That's got nothing to do with it.

JURGEN: I'd be long gone if I were you.

FATHER: You don't know that Jurg.

JURGEN: You've always been a weak twerp. That Leo Beumer that you remember, I've never known him. He never existed. *(Meanwhile takes a photo album out of the rucksack, rips a page out, tears up all the photos.)*

FATHER: Are you completely mad! Els!

MOTHER: *(To FATHER.)* The longer this goes on the greater the chance that this will be a traumatic experience for them. *(Walks over to Esther.)*

JURGEN: *(Meanwhile ripping up the photo album.)*

MOTHER: *(Has meanwhile taken the key off of ESTHER, makes the shutters roll up again.)*

ESTHER: You said you'd help me Jurg!

JURGEN: He's got to go Es. The whole thing's got to burst, you can feel it all around. *(Ripping up photos.)* Everything's got to be smashed Els, you know that.

FATHER: You can't do that Jurg. That's a whole life.

JURGEN: It's not my life.

FATHER: *(Walks over to JURGEN.)* Jurg. Fucking hell-

JURGEN: I don't know these people, I've never met them.

FATHER: *(Tries to hold JURGEN back.)*

JURGEN: Look at these stupid smiles. They're all pulling the same face in every photo.

VOICE OF AUNTIE THEA: *(Has continued counting in the meantime.)* 24, 23, 22, 21-

FATHER: *(Shouts.)* I can't leave now Thea-

VOICE OF AUNTIE THEA: Nonsense-

JURGEN: *(Shouts.)* He's on his way!

FATHER: Shut up boy.

ESTHER: Daddy!

FATHER: Fucking hell!

VOICE OF AUNTIE THEA: 16, 15, 14, 13-

JURGEN: He's on his way!

ESTHER: Jurg!

> *(FATHER puts his hand over JURGEN's mouth.)*

VOICE OF AUNTIE THEA: 10, 9, 8, 7-

JURGEN: *(Bites FATHER's hand.)*

FATHER: Ow! *(Lets go of JURGEN.)*

VOICE OF AUNTIE THEA: *(Has continued counting in the meantime.)* 4, 3, 2-

JURGEN: *(Shouts into the intercom.)* He's on his way! *(He pushes ESTHER away, she's trying to turn the key again.)*

VOICE OF AUNTIE THEA: *(Meanwhile.)* 1- 0.

JURGEN: *(Shouts.)* He's on his way now. Just hang on. Auntie Thea!

> *We hear a car door slam and a car drive away, silence, FATHER quickly rescues the photo albums.*

JURGEN: Missed chance Leo Beumer. Missed chance Es. Els-

> *MOTHER fetches the vacuum cleaner, starts vacuuming. ESTHER, JURGEN and FATHER watch Mother in amazement.*

BLACK OUT

> *The table is more or less laid again. The family is seated at the table. **MOTHER** is eating, the rest of the family don't know what to do with themselves.*

MOTHER: Hey guys. Can you imagine that I was born exactly forty-five years ago. *(Looks at her watch).* Honestly, forty-five years to the minute. It was such a clear day. Just like today. And there was a thick carpet of snow on the ground. My father had had to dig the car out every morning for a whole week long, just in case I arrived. Everywhere people were skating. Rosy cheeks, frozen faces. Little stalls selling hot chocolate, doughnuts. My father and mother by the stove. And every now and then they'd go and look at my little room. It was all completely ready. With a changing table and a little bath. A music-box above the cradle.

> ***ESTHER** and **JURGEN** start packing their rucksack.*

MOTHER: Just ignore it Leo. *(Cheerfully.)* It was so terribly cold, the night I was born. I could hear my mother's teeth chattering. My father cursing because the roads were so slippery.

FATHER: Els-

MOTHER: *(Sharply.)* We're not going to react Leo- *(Continues resolutely.)* And we hadn't even got inside the maternity clinic and I'd almost arrived. They had to put another woman who'd been pushing for hours back to bed. Because I so wanted to be born, guys, I so terribly wanted to be born. And I was so welcome. I was so terribly welcome.

> ***ESTHER** and **JURGEN** exit, silence*

FATHER: *(After a little while puts his coat on.)*

MOTHER: Take that coat off Leo.

FATHER: But-

MOTHER: That's exactly what they want. Take that coat off.

FATHER: *(Takes his coat off, sits down again.)*

MOTHER: It's just <u>one</u> big cry for attention.

-END-

SENSE

by Anja Hilling
Translated by Logan Kennedy and Leonhard Unglaub

Further Copyright Information

Sense

Characters

PHÖBE

FRED

TOMMI

KARL

JULE

JASMIN

ALBERT

NATASCHA

BEATE

LAURENT

FIRST PERFORMED IN THE UK ON 27TH APRIL, 2009,
AT SOUTHWARK PLAYHOUSE, LONDON.

I. EYES

Phöbe and Fred

1.

FRED: Phöbe's eyes are blue.
Only sometimes. In certain conditions.
Sun fever and also fear.
That's when her eyes suddenly turn turquoise.

PHÖBE: It's true. But Fred. He only knows this because he's heard people say so.

FRED: But it's true.

PHÖBE: Yes.

2.

FRED: A garden party.
It's high summer. August.
It's Tommi's birthday.
Tommi invited her.
Tommi. Finally.
He said. I'm turning eighteen on Friday.
Fred's going to be the DJ. That's what he said. In the garden around nine. And bring one of your girlfriends.
She knew the facts.
About the party the time.
That they were still short of girls.
She knew that Tommi's father was a baker.
Had turned his bakery into a franchise with three branches. Had a
home with a garden and a platinum blonde girlfriend.
She knew that Tommi had started smoking a year earlier.
That Tommi had lost his best friend that year. Karl.
That Tommi once hit a girl. Jasmin.
Karl had only been a familiar face to her. Jasmin she only knew from gym class.
But she knew. There was a secret with Tommi. And a sadness.

And she liked that very much.
She knew a few things about Tommi.
But she'd never heard of Fred.

PHÖBE: Tommi touched my arm.
He touched my arm and invited me.

FRED: Phöbe had played it all out in her mind.
A thousand times.
Only a little more spectacular.
She talked with Tommi about everything.
About school smoking sadness.
About everything on every level from every perspective.
Swimming as moonlight guests in the Teufelssee.
Walking on sand.
Breathless after a fall into the January snow.
He compared her eyes with the lake in which they swam.
Her skin with the snow in which they lay.
And she.
She then put her fingers on his lips.
And he always.
He always kissed her like no one else could.
Tommi.
When he'd invited her she was a little disappointed.
With his sweaty fingers and his dirty nails.
She had also imagined his voice differently.
And then he flicked his cigarette butt onto her shoe.

PHÖBE: He didn't mean to.

FRED: That's the way it is with daydream friends.

PHÖBE: I did what I could.
For three months I never had more than two pimples on my face.
Never more than five of my back.
It took seven months for my hair to grow to its party length.
I put a single blonde streak in my bangs.
Red T-shirt white jeans.
I looked like strawberry ice cream.
I had wanted Tommi for such a long time.
I wanted to be with him.
For everyone to see.

Eternally.
I knew it would be different.
Different from what I thought.
But that would be good too.
I really wanted it.
To become real between Tommi and me.

FRED: She didn't see Fred coming. She didn't even know about him.

PHÖBE: If I had.
Had known about him.
I wouldn't have been interested in him.
With his skinny arms his stupid blond ponytail.
Neigh.
Someone should let him know.
That his pony tail looks like shit.
He has no idea.

3.

FRED: Before Tommi opens the door Phöbe sees her collar bone gleaming in the front door's little window.
Tommi has a bun in his hand and she can smell sausage on his breath.
He says. Hello Beate.

PHÖBE: I'd brought Beate along.
She comes in handy on occasions like these.
She likes to sit in the corner alone smokes pot without tobacco.
She doesn't want to hang out with me and I don't want to hang out with her.
And that's something we both respect.
She didn't even notice that Tommi said hello to her first.

FRED: When Phöbe is alone with Tommi for a moment she tries to start a conversation.

PHÖBE: So this is your home is it.

FRED: Nice. She says.

PHÖBE: Luxurious.

FRED: Tommi says. Come on in. Or else go outside. The party's outside. I've got to get to the barbeque.

PHÖBE: Tommi has to go turn the cutlets.

FRED: He is where he always is.
Miles away from her.
He's standing among the guests smoking without a filter.
His eyes in line with his fingers.
It's an image Phöbe's familiar with.
She thinks it's sad and also beautiful.
That's just the way he stands.
On the schoolyard at the kiosk in the subway.
Now he's standing here and there's no difference at all.
Phöbe closes her eyes and spirits him away.
Away from the barbecue from the guests.
Towards her.
When Tommi actually does start moving in her direction.
She begins noticing the music for the first time.
My music.

4.

PHÖBE: Electronic. Slow.
The DJ is standing at the decks under the chestnut tree.
I really like the music.

FRED: Tommi isn't going towards Phöbe.
He's going to his father.

PHÖBE: The baker is standing behind me.
He's calling something across the garden.
A name.

FRED: My name.

PHÖBE: Fred.

FRED: I smile. He's my uncle.
Smiling is what you do.

PHÖBE: The DJ's eyes are directed above us.
High above us.

I'm thinking.
Maybe he's standing on a root.

FRED: As I raise my glass in my uncle's direction.
That's when Phöbe remembers it's Tommi's birthday.

PHÖBE: I really put some thought into it.
At first I thought a book.
Maybe Dostoyevsky.
Then.
A gift certificate.
Theatre.
Maybe he likes that kind of thing.
Now I have a bottle in my bag.
Tequila. Brown.
Four oranges and some cinnamon too.

FRED: The baker leaves and Phöbe. Phöbe has Tommi behind her. She stretches her head. Lengthens her neck and spine and very softly turns around.

PHÖBE: I turn around and Tommi is doing something else.

FRED: Making buns for the party.

PHÖBE: He takes out the dough. Kneads it. Then starts throwing small balls of it at the DJ. The DJ doesn't move. He's under attack and doesn't even flinch.

FRED: It's just dough. Dough doesn't stink doesn't hurt.

PHÖBE: One ball falls into the hollow of his elbow. He lets it stay there. For a bit. Then he eats it.

FRED: What were you thinking at the time.

PHÖBE: I was thinking. Gentle. He's gentle. But his hair looks like shit.

FRED: When she gives Tommi the bottle. He says. Tequila is good.

PHÖBE: Tequila is one thing that's always missing. He says.

FRED: She leaves the oranges and cinnamon in her bag.

5.

PHÖBE: Tommi goes away. But only to fix a plate of food for me. Cutlets and sausages.

FRED: Him fixing her a plate. It should have made her happy. She had never been so close to her dream.

PHÖBE: But I'm not happy. I don't know what's happened. The music has changed. The melody of the bass. A string of lights flashes on in the chestnut tree. I look over. I think. So that's Fred is it. His face is blue. From the light of the screen. But his eyes are not looking at it. They're peering above the screen above the folding chairs. His eyes could even make it over the hedge to the neighbour's property. If I weren't standing here. Being hit. By the silent stretch of his gaze. He's not smiling. Not moving. Only his fingers are moving sliders up and down. His eyes are bright and cold.

FRED: Tommi's coming back with cutlets.

PHÖBE: I'll get you some sausage later. He says.

FRED: But you. You're looking at me. Not at him.

PHÖBE: You're the one who's looking at me. What a stare. Makes me sick.

FRED: You took the plate anyway.

PHÖBE: So that's Fred is it. I say to Tommi. How do you know each other. I ask him. And Tommi. Tommi laughs.

FRED: He's my cousin. Tommi says. We're related what were you thinking.

PHÖBE: I'm thinking he takes himself for a hero standing there on his root like that. Your cousin. I think he's staring at me. That's what I tell Tommi. Seriously.

FRED: Tommi laughs. He says. Sure. Fred is staring at you. Then he takes her by the hand and that. That wasn't the way it was supposed to be. His grip too limp. A stringy bit of cutlet between her teeth. She should be happy. But she's only being introduced to someone.

PHÖBE: Fred.

6.

FRED: Tommi says. Fred. This is Phöbe. And I.

PHÖBE: You smile. Your smile is blue behind your computer.
Now you're looking down not up high anymore. As if
you're tired or shy. I've never seen anybody like you
before. I can't believe that you're not looking at me.
Now. When it would be okay. I can't stop staring at
your eyelashes. Thick and light. Rabbit's lashes.

FRED: Tommi says. Phöbe thinks you're staring at her.
But really. Says Tommi. Really she's the one who's
staring at you.

PHÖBE: And that. That makes you so proud.

FRED: Yeah.

PHÖBE: He lifts his eyes. Fred does.
And the stillness of his eyes flows and undulates
behind my temples.
I feel like puking.
I chuck the bone from my cutlet down at the trunk of
the chestnut tree.
Is he blind or something.
Are you blind or something.

FRED: Tommi leaves.
He says. I'll leave you two alone.
Phöbe sees him take something out of his pocket. A
cigarette or a bun she couldn't care less.
She's looking at me.
She puts her hand on my arm. Firmly not tenderly.
Her fingers are greasy her voice loud.

PHÖBE: So is this what you guys find funny.
This is your kind of humour.

FRED: Just leave me alone for a minute. Okay.
Phöbe.

PHÖBE: He says my name. And his voice is friendly.

FRED: Can you get me something from the barbecue.
You see I wouldn't find my way.

PHÖBE: I don't believe a word you're saying.

FRED: She takes a step towards me.
She's close to me. So close her breath sweeps through
my
eyelashes.

PHÖBE:	What colour's my T-shirt.
FRED:	I'm DJing. I'm busy.
PHÖBE:	Good luck with the barbeque.
FRED:	Red.
PHÖBE:	Exactly. Red you idiot.
FRED:	Red like love roses tomatoes. That's what I've been told.
PHÖBE:	Fuck off.
FRED:	You fuck off.
PHÖBE:	My T-shirt is red.
FRED:	I guessed.
PHÖBE:	You're not being funny.
FRED:	What more do you need. A dog a cane. A computer that talks to me.
PHÖBE:	You're blind. You really are blind.
FRED:	I'm going to be DJing tomorrow at the Bergdorf.
PHÖBE:	Where's that.
FRED:	Why would you ask me.
PHÖBE:	Kiss my ass.
FRED:	Are you coming.
PHÖBE:	No.
FRED:	You definitely have to come.
PHÖBE:	Whether I come or not. You wouldn't recognize me anyway.
FRED:	You could say hello.
PHÖBE:	Hello.
FRED:	I would always recognize you.
PHÖBE:	What colour are my eyes.
FRED:	No idea.

7.

PHÖBE: My eyes are blue. Sometimes turquoise. They're jewels
my eyes. They're an absolute must see. They're the
most beautiful thing about me. Always have been.
Even when I still had pimples and greasy hair and was
fatter. Even then they sparkled in my face. Promised
me beauty. Forced me to believe in fairy tale wisdom.
Princess. Every fairy tale needs its bad phases.
Phases. Where beauty takes its time. To move from
the inside to the outside. That's the way they are. My
eyes. Blue turquoise and full of promise.
Fred. He doesn't even know this.
The whole world catches on my eyes.
Is drawn in by the ocean beam and he.
He says. Blue.
Blue as the sky blue as smurfs as ground fire.
At least he's never said blue food.
And turquoise.
Turquoise is hard to describe that's as far as we go.
No further.
My eyes are beautiful.
They're wasted on him.
His eyes.
I tell him. Blaring. Almost colourless.
If you want to know. Ash blue pigeon blue almost grey.
He's disappointed.
I lied.
What I really wanted to say.
I wanted to say. Your eyes are bright.
Brighter than mine brighter than light.
Your eyes are the brightest thing I've ever seen.
They don't draw me in.
They light me up. Light everything up.
I wanted to say. With you I'd stop being afraid of the
dark.
Because you would illuminate any path in the woods
any basement
any heart.
I wanted to say something like that.

I don't know what got into me.
Maybe I was feeling my cold coming on already.
It wasn't something I wanted imagined wished for.
But I knew I would be there tomorrow.
Where he was DJing.

8.

FRED: Seriously
She was there.
At the Bergdorf.
And I didn't even notice.
I just heard about it much later.
Too late to be happy about it.

PHÖBE: It's crowded.
First I see Beate.
She's kissing a guy with yellow hair.
Her skin is white his is dark.
It's a beautiful kiss.
Calm.
It goes against the music.
Against the movement in the room.
Their eyes closed.
When Beate opens her eyes she'll be surprised.
She won't see me.
Not in this corner.
I'm looking at Fred.
He's standing on some root again.
His head slanted.
Light in his rabbit's eyelashes.
I'm standing still.
I imagine the opposite.
Undressing myself.
Dancing naked to his music.
Wild pirouettes.
People might laugh at me.
Scream. Or applaud. He would wonder about all the
noise.
Wouldn't know it was me.

Later.
When he'd hear about it.
How I danced.
How I was raped.
Or taken into custody.
Maybe he'd be surprised.
Later.
Never right away.
First he'd make a smooth transition.
From one song to the next.
His ponytail touching the corner of his mouth.
Kissing Fred.
It's impossible.
It's something he'll never experience.
The surprise about my face being there after the kiss.
I want to go look at him.
One last look.
Then get the hell out of here.
He's holding his head straight now and his eyes hit
me.
Straight across the room between my eyebrows.
A bright beam presses me to the wall.
The wall is moist.
The sweat from the ceiling.
I'm cold.
Beate starts talking to me.
Beate says. You look like shit Phöbe.
She thinks I'm getting sick.
A new song is starting.

9.

FRED: When she looks in the mirror that night.
         The skin covering her limbs is thin.
         Her head is heavy and her eyes.
         They're turquoise.

PHÖBE: My cold comes the next morning right after the club.

FRED:	She's almost relieved about the congestion in her nose. The high digit the thermometer climbs to she finds factual and beautiful. Her mouth is dry her skin hot. She can hardly open her eyes and she's cold. She sleeps all day and through the next night too.
PHÖBE:	The morning after that. Two days after the Bergdorf. Three days after Tommi's party Fred calls me.
FRED:	How are you.
PHÖBE:	I recognized his voice right away. Who's this.
FRED:	It's me Fred.
PHÖBE:	Oh.
FRED:	Too bad you weren't there. At the Bergdorf.
PHÖBE:	Yeah. Too bad.
FRED:	Otherwise. Are you doing well.
PHÖBE:	No. Otherwise I feel like shit.
FRED:	I'll drop by.
PHÖBE:	No.
FRED:	I'll be there in an hour.
PHÖBE:	No. You'll just catch my cold.
FRED:	Okay. See you in a bit.
PHÖBE:	No.
FRED:	She's almost yelling. She's afraid.
PHÖBE:	No.
FRED:	Don't worry. I'll use my cane.
PHÖBE:	Then the nausea comes back. In the next hour I puke twice into the sink and once into the toilet.

10.

FRED:	She lets me in.
PHÖBE:	I don't know what's gotten into me. I'm alone. My father's gone. My mother is off selling flowers at the

organic market. He's nineteen. He's got a cane. He
could be dangerous. If only by accident. I let him in.

FRED: You really are feeling shitty.

PHÖBE: He has no idea.

FRED: Do you look as miserable as you smell.

PHÖBE: Piss off I'm feeling just dandy.

FRED: You should get to bed.

PHÖBE: Right. And you're coming with me I suppose.

FRED: Yeah. Of course.

PHÖBE: He's holding the cane folded in his hand.

11.

FRED: Nine hours.

PHÖBE: For nine hours he sat at my bedside.
At some point I smell oranges.
I open my eyes. They're crusted over.
Behind the crusty veil I see Fred.
With small clean teeth he's taking the white skin off
the peeled fruit.

FRED: Vitamins.

PHÖBE: Your ponytail looks like shit.
Don't you have someone who tells you that kind of
thing.

FRED: Here. Eat.

PHÖBE: You brought oranges just for me. Lucky me.
Have you fallen in love or something.

FRED: Or something. She asks.

PHÖBE: Does it happen that quickly with you guys.
A voice a name an orange.
You're getting a little carried away with your
imagination.
Maybe. There are no limits to your imagination.
But I am where it stops. Here and now.
You're blind for Christ's sake. You don't know who I
am.

You wouldn't recognize me at the train station.
I could dye my hair. Wear neon.
I could kiss somebody else right in front of your eyes.
I could be ugly as the night. It wouldn't matter to you.
But I'm not. I'm not ugly.
I'm even pretty attractive and it feels good.
To hear that every once in a while you know.
From someone who knows about these things.
Someone. Who can say. My girlfriend. She is the most beautiful
woman in the world.
Someone. Who you'd believe when he says that kind of thing.
People would laugh about you. About us. Sorry.
We'd be cartoon characters. Popeye and Olive.
I don't need that. Really I don't. I don't need you. I'm sorry.
Please get lost. Okay.
Clear out get your cane tapping rig up your dog.
And thanks for the vitamins.

FRED: I think she's not looking at me.

12.

PHÖBE: He drops the oranges on my duvet.

FRED: It's not like I went out of my way to bring you them.
Your mother found them in your bag.

PHÖBE: You talked to my mother.

FRED: I'm leaving.

PHÖBE: He's leaving. He's already at the door.
He's got his cane strapped to his belt at his hip.
He looks amazing to me there at the door. Daring.
He reminds me of everything that's dangerous and beautiful in the world.
Wild West duels speeding dying for love.
Don't go.
I'm sorry.
I didn't mean it. What I just said.

FRED: Of course. Of course you meant it. What you just said.
It's not a bad thing.
Taking a position.
It's a starting point.

PHÖBE: It's bullshit. Not a position.

FRED: It doesn't happen that quickly.
I'm not in love with you.
We don't fall in love that quickly.

13.

PHÖBE: Of course I meant everything I said.
Each word came from my heart.
And I never said it was good my heart or special.
It's just a heart. It just shoots things out.
And then turns into a liar and says.
Oh I didn't mean it. What I said.
I was confused. I still am.
He's blind.
And it's absolutely. In every respect idiotic.
To have a blind admirer.
It's not worth shit. Or at least not much. My body
would be insulted. My friends amused my eyes
confused. I'd no longer be able to recognize myself.
I would see myself with his eyes. His eyes. Because
that's the way it is. When you're in love with someone
you see with their eyes and that. That would be too
bad. If all I'm seeing here. Were to vanish from one
day to the next. Into thin air. Fantasy. Just because
my lover has no eyes. I mean. It's something. Really
something that you can spend a thought or two on.
That can confuse you. Because despite all the waste in
this. You wish for nothing more than a phone call. To
hear his voice. That would be a start.

FRED: She waits two days. Then she calls me.

14.

PHÖBE: He says my name

FRED:	Phöbe. She closes her eyes on the phone.
PHÖBE:	I'm feeling better.
FRED:	Good.
PHÖBE:	Yeah. How about you.
FRED:	Me. I'd like to see you.
PHÖBE:	You idiot.
FRED:	I'm serious.
PHÖBE:	Me too.
FRED:	When.
PHÖBE:	Today. Now.
FRED:	Yeah. Now.
PHÖBE:	What do you want to do.
FRED:	Whatever.
PHÖBE:	Pause.
	There's an interruption. A pain in the sole of my foot. He doesn't know if I'm still on the line.
FRED:	Hello.
PHÖBE:	What do you mean whatever. In our situation you have to spend a thought or two on it. On what you want to do and what you don't want to do. Should we go to the movies or something. Or is having half the fun not worth our money. What about the zoo. It's acoustically interesting and we can go to the petting zoo that's better.
FRED:	Whatever you want. If you want to go to the movies. We can go to the movies. Only knobs go to the movies in the summer but we can go great idea.
PHÖBE:	In the end only his breath.
FRED:	We don't hang up. We could. But we don't.
PHÖBE:	Whatever. Let's just do something. I want to see you.
FRED:	She's smiling on the phone. Let's go swimming.
PHÖBE:	What.

FRED: We are going to the lake. We'll take the train see you in a bit.

15.

PHÖBE: I lied twice for my date at the lake. I told my mother I was going to a friend's. I told my friend I was helping my mother make bouquets. I tiptoe towards the train station. He has both his hands crossed over his cane in front of his body. His legs twisted as if in a dance. When he's ten yards from me. I think of turning around. Saying nothing just leaving and forgetting him. Then it's too late. He turns around.

FRED: You're late.

PHÖBE: I take his hand. I don't know why. You just forget yourself sometimes. I don't know how you did that.

FRED: Did what.

PHÖBE: I can feel his hand. Stronger now.
He increases the pressure.
Initiates a wave that travels through my arms my shoulders my neck.
A twitching under my eyelids a pressure on my temples just shy of pain.
From my mouth a sound. A vowel.
I let go of his hand.
Right away.

FRED: You don't know how I did what.

PHÖBE: How you knew I was here.
I was way too far away.

FRED: You were late.
I thought now she might come.
And there you were.
So it was a matter of luck.
Don't get carried away.

PHÖBE: Isn't there something. Something about me.
That you notice more than with other people.
My smell my breath the way I walk.

FRED: We don't know each other that well yet.

PHÖBE:	Exactly.
FRED:	Exactly.
PHÖBE:	Then he takes me in his arms. I feel his breath in my ear his cane against my spine. The train is late.

16.

FRED:	We didn't say a word to each other the whole way. She looked me in the face and I. I don't know what she saw there or found there. All I know is that. That it was like she was entering me. Like fear or drugs or pain. Extreme. And also beautiful. And suddenly you wish the train trip would never end. And then you pull into station. Come on. Come on let's go swimming. It's fucking hot in here. But she. She trips over her own towel. And bangs her head against the handrail. For an instant the world goes black before her eyes. As they say. And her knees buckle. Are you alright.
PHÖBE:	That's just what happens when.
FRED:	When what.
PHÖBE:	When I look at you too long.
FRED:	Then look somewhere else.
PHÖBE:	I can't.
FRED:	Why not.
PHÖBE:	I think you're. I don't know. Somehow. Somehow I think you're incredibly beautiful.
FRED:	Come on let's go swimming.
PHÖBE:	So now you're shy are you.

FRED: So now you're in love are you.

17.

PHÖBE: That's right. The whole way I looked into his face.
Lost myself in his eyes for more than forty minutes.
And it wasn't like looking into anyone else's eyes. It
was different. It was one-way. No back and forth. No
exchange. Nothing came back at me. And I didn't
notice a single one of the stops the train made. I'm
not lying that's the way it was. I was inside his eye-
sockets. Disappeared into them for forty minutes. I
didn't see anything there or else I forgot everything. I
haven't the faintest clue what goes on in there. But I
was there. Happily. And then full of rage. I find you
excessive in your blindness. Unreachable exaggerated
an overdose. Awful. Helpless and unspeakably elegant.
I see you beneath the stars zipping headlong through
a universe. Then tripping over the curb. Your hand that
always misses. Your hand in my bloodstream. Your
foot in the gap between train and platform. I see you
stumbling through the night. Falling over stones on the
way to the lake. Gliding through the Milky Way. I want
to be close to you. Closer.
I want to know how much more there is.
Behind your eyes.
I have a thousand questions.
Is it bright or dark your world.
Does music move inside you.
Like a snake maybe or like a spider or something.
Do noises have a smell and what about me.
Can you smell me.
Am I a colour a sound a movement.
Am I three-dimensional.
What do you think when you hear my voice.
Do you imagine me. Have an image.
Where would it come from.
Do you even know what that is. An image.
Or is there just a desert inside you.
Where nothing can grow.

I really want to know that want to see that.
The landscape behind your eyes.
I want to see what you see.
See myself with your eyes.
Whiz through your eyeballs.
Explode into your universe.
Be inside you shine and scream.

FRED: Come on let's go swimming. It's fucking hot in here.

PHÖBE: Then I blacked out.

II. Nose

Tommi and Karl

1.

KARL: You're a smoker.

TOMMI: And you're dead.

KARL: Man quit this ghost crap.

TOMMI: Then get out of here.

KARL: Can I have a drag.

2.

KARL: Smack in the middle of summer the first box. Red Gauloises. In October the blue ones. Since January he's been rolling his own.

TOMMI: What do you know about it.

KARL: At first he inhaled the smoke. A quick draw. Then he spit it back out into the room. Later he was able to keep it in the hollow of his mouth. And let it out again. A white ribbon. After four weeks he was able to draw the nicotine through his lungs. Split the smoke in two with his nostrils. At first the idea was to smoke out the room.

TOMMI: But that wasn't enough.

KARL: It was inside him not in the room. An evil spell. A visitation. A smell. Every single night.

TOMMI: I wanted to be able to sleep again. That's all. To have my peace and quiet.

KARL: Hence the chain smoking.

TOMMI: The smell of the magic is sour and sweet.

KARL: Sweet as blood. Sour as bread.

TOMMI: Night after night he's standing in front of me. Karl. As if he still possessed it all. A smell a face this fucking corpse.

KARL: That's the way it is with friends.
          They don't leave each other.

3.

TOMMI: We were friends.

KARL: Are.

TOMMI: Were.

KARL: Are.

TOMMI: To me you've been long dead.

KARL: It's always been like that.
          Best friends.
          As they say.
          Ever since we learned to talk to walk to think.

TOMMI: The same kindergarten the same school.
          Everything the same.
          Even our taste.
          In sneakers movies women.

KARL: The same hair style.

TOMMI: Karl blond.

KARL: Tommi brown.

TOMMI: Even our birthdays are on the same day.

KARL: August twelfth.

TOMMI: Karl's father had a stroke.

KARL: Tommi's had a bakery.
          Later even three.

TOMMI: Karl's mother just couldn't cope with all the work.

KARL: Tommi's is dead.
          She's baking stars now.
          After a year the baker found himself a Greek woman.
          For his bed his heart his oven.

TOMMI: Helena.

KARL: She. This Greek woman. Was like a mother to both of
          us.

4.

TOMMI: We were eight. My mother had been dead a year and the Greek woman. She had dark heavy curls. Her body was small and soft and her eyes black. I thought. Now. Now the tender part of life begins. The Greek woman's armpits smelled of goat's milk. She loved the bakery. The early hours the warmth of the oven and the rising yeast. And Karl and I. We loved the Greek woman.

KARL: But the only German words that ever came from her mouth. Were bakery words. Tommi's father waited eight months for a conversation. Then he began to use a different language. Tommi found her. Her face stuck to the oven window. You could peel her skin off from her temples to her ear. Tommi wanted to go to her. Comfort her. With familiar words.

TOMMI: Broetchen Guglhupf Schrippen Schnecken.

KARL: His father tore him away from her and he found himself. With his face in the warm yeasty dough. The dough grew larger and rounder. Grew around his face. He imagined dying like that. His nose clogged up with yeast. But that's not what happened. He was saved and the Greek woman too. Two cousins took her back to Athens. Tommi never saw Helena again.

TOMMI: But I have her inside me. In my nose my brain. All that yeast. I know it's going to grow. As yeast does. And one day it'll burst me open from the inside.

KARL: The bakery was renamed. It was now called Helena's.

TOMMI: When we turned fifteen my father gave Karl a job. Three days a week after school. As a baking assistant at Helena's.

KARL: I had the same longing for the Greek woman.

TOMMI: You don't even know what that is. Longing. For you it could be for a cookie. A joint a chocolate heart.

KARL: When we turned sixteen. Last August. I baked a marble cake at Helena's.
With two grams of hash in it for Tommi and me.

TOMMI: And I. I met Jasmin.

5.

KARL: Tommi loved Jasmin. Right from the beginning. Like mad. He told everyone. Me included. About her hair. Which was light red and wavy. Her hazel eyes. Her eyebrows.

TOMMI: Poured into her face like a liqueur.

KARL: And her body. Which was like her hair.

TOMMI: Long and wavy.

KARL: Her breath. She made this rasping sound and sometimes rattled. Just like that. Then she'd hold a puffer to her lips. Which would rattle too.

TOMMI: She had emphysema. A congenital enzyme deficiency.

KARL: Tommi even loved that about her. That she shot cortisone into her lungs.

TOMMI: She put the spray to her lips. And I thought. Maybe it will sound like that. When she kisses me.

KARL: On the bus to school he told her everything. Laid out the facts. Why he loved her.

TOMMI: She was very quiet.

KARL: She was flattered.

TOMMI: She gave me her number.

KARL: She was fifteen. She had only dreamt about speeches like that.

TOMMI: She gave me her number.

KARL: They went out. Tommi and Jasmin. Movies clubs the zoo the things people do. He really held on to her. Put his nose to her. As if they were dogs terrified of going home.

TOMMI: Her ears lemon. Her neck coriander. Her lower arms wet meadow her upper arms bearskin.

KARL: He was infatuated almost drunk. He felt that her smell was filling him up. That the yeast inside him was shrinking. That it would soon disappear into the landscape of her skin.

TOMMI: I was in awe.

KARL: He marvelled at her. Like you marvel at some phenomenon. A natural wonder. To him she was a mountain. Reddish-yellow and strange.

TOMMI: You didn't know her. Not like I did.

KARL: You were crazy.

TOMMI: You don't know what that means. To be crazy for someone. You go down on your knees. You pray with your arms wide open. That's how crazy I was for her.

KARL: It was your own feeling you were crazy for. As for her. You pretty much forgot her in the midst of it.

TOMMI: I didn't touch her.

KARL: You pestered her.

TOMMI: I didn't touch her. She said. I've got emphysema. Sex cigarettes and sports. It's all poison to me. You've got to be careful. Careful. If you know what that means.

KARL: I know you were crazy.

TOMMI: Yeah. You knew everything. I told you everything. That's what friends are for.

6.

KARL: I knew everything. And still fell in love with Jasmin.

TOMMI: In April. In my father's bakery.
You don't know what it's like.
To lose everything.
In the middle of spring.
Any sense to keep on breathing.

KARL: She was sweet. Her hair moist. Her skin gleamed and smelled of sweat. She said. I'm back from volleyball and need some bread.

TOMMI: Volleyball. You're so full of shit. We're talking about Jasmin here. She doesn't stress her lungs with team sports.

KARL: The volleyball business was a lie. She had wetted her hair and moistened her lips next door at the espresso bar. Ran twenty yards. Which was enough to make her skin sweaty. I only found out later. About the lie. About the effort she put into making this first entrance.

TOMMI: Stop it.

KARL: When I gave her the buns she touched my hand.

TOMMI: No she didn't. You grabbed her. By the fucking hand.

KARL: I even told her to say hello. Say hello to Tommi for me. I don't know why. I thought that's what people do.

TOMMI: Say hello to Tommi for me. You asshole.

KARL: When I said that. She lifted our hands with the bag of buns to my lips.

TOMMI: Your hands. I'm going to puke.

KARL: Then she kissed me.

TOMMI: She kissed you.

KARL: And I kissed her.

TOMMI: You asshole. I'll never forgive you for that.

KARL: Her lips smelled of yeast.
I thought. Maybe just this morning she'd seen Tommi.
I thought. Maybe you had kissed.
I thought of you. You asshole.
When I kissed her.
It was a bit like kissing you.

TOMMI: You fucking homo. That's no way to ask for forgiveness.

7.

KARL: Jasmin split up with Tommi right away. That same night. Tommi couldn't believe his ears.

TOMMI: There must have been a misunderstanding a mistake an error. We were at the beginning not the end. She didn't know what she was doing. What she was saying. She didn't know the meaning of it. Love. What you stand to lose. Everything. Otherwise she would have known how to feel. Like me. Like being stuck in a heap of shit. A fly in the steam of her shit. God I love her.

KARL: Tommi told me about it. On the phone.

8.

TOMMI: I feel it again. This fear.

KARL: What fear.

TOMMI: I can smell it. It's not gone. It's everywhere. It's inside me.

KARL: Will you quit this shit about the yeast.

TOMMI: She's with someone else. Someone else. Let's have a good laugh my friend.

KARL: But I heard him scream. Sob and whimper on the phone. He threw the receiver to the floor. I landed on a soft carpet. I said his name. Tommi.
Twice.
Tommi.
I felt like hanging up after the third time.
I wanted to think about Jasmin.
About her moist skin after volleyball.
I didn't mean to but I couldn't help smiling.

TOMMI: Karl.

KARL: There he was again. Tommi my boy.

TOMMI: Karl. What am I supposed to do.

KARL: No idea. Call her.

TOMMI: Call her. You think I didn't already do that eleven times. Do you think she'd pick up.

KARL: Then go look for her.

TOMMI: Yeah. Let's go look for her. Great idea Karl. Where could she be. Let's do some thinking here. The guy. Where could he be. Where does one hang out. When one's existence is an absolute error. Where do you live. When you're an absolute misunderstanding. Just let me know Karl. And I'm there.

KARL: Maybe she's playing volleyball.

TOMMI: Volleyball. I'm going to be sick.

KARL: Then go puke.

TOMMI: You hung up.

KARL: I didn't want it to be like that.

TOMMI: That was okay with me. If I was going to be alone then at least totally alone.

KARL: I didn't want it to be like that.

9.

TOMMI: Karl didn't want it to be like that. He wanted to call Jasmin. To say. It won't work.

KARL: Because of Tommi. It was nice but it won't work I'm sorry.

TOMMI: But he didn't say anything like that.

KARL: I'm sorry.

TOMMI: He asked the baker. My father. If he could stay on. After closing time.

KARL: I'd like to try out a recipe.

TOMMI: A recipe. That's what he called it. My father the baker was thrilled.

KARL: Jasmin said yes. Right away. I invited her. To come to the bakery after closing time and she. She said yes. Simple as that.

TOMMI: Yeah. Even though she definitely knew. What kind of a dark and dusty room it is. The bakehouse.

KARL: She wasn't stupid. You and I had been friends forever. She knew you. She knew. Either here or not at all. But then there was more light than she'd expected.

TOMMI: The sheen of the baking equipment. The white flour dust the gray laminate floor. The air heavy and sweet. Makes you faint air like that. A braided yeast loaf was glowing in the oven. That is so fucked up. Baking her a braided loaf like that.

KARL: When she was standing in front of me. In the dark of the bakery. To me there was nothing in the world. That could have been whiter. Than the white of her eye.

TOMMI: You are staring at her. In this flour dust hell. And already she can't breathe through the nose.

KARL: Her puffer stayed in her bag.

TOMMI: You two are killing me. Every part of me.

KARL: We tasted the braided loaf.

It had turned out too dark and too salty.

TOMMI: She said it was good anyway.

KARL: She said. It tastes like shit.

TOMMI: Then you fucked her.

She could hardly breathe. And you fucked her.

KARL: I touched her face. Her mouth smiled her teeth gleamed. Warmth flowed into my nose. A nosebleed flowing backwards.

TOMMI: They lay down on the table. The table. Where my father rolls out the dough shapes buns braids pretzels.

KARL: Her skin was warm and salty. I was happy in that place.

TOMMI: She had to cough.

KARL: I think she was a little afraid.

TOMMI: A little afraid.

KARL: I was afraid too.

TOMMI: She hurt herself on the table.

KARL: We felt it all. Wood skin flour. Everywhere. Between our shoulder blades. Toes. Fingers. In the hollows of our knees. We shared that. The fear and the pain.

TOMMI: You don't even know what that means. To be sharing something.

KARL: It was beautiful.

TOMMI: Afterwards you whispered in her ear. That was so beautiful.

KARL: We didn't say a word to each other.

TOMMI: You never shared anything with anyone.

10.

KARL: Tommi spent that night in front of Jasmin's house.
           Wearing a green leather jacket and a yellow T-shirt.
           Leaning on a red Mercedes.
           He looked like a set of traffic lights.
           Except a little mixed up.

TOMMI: I didn't want to scare her didn't hide myself. Wanted
           her to see me. Right away. I just wanted to talk with
           her.

KARL: You wanted to tell her that she was a miracle not a
           human being.

TOMMI: A volcano between row-houses. A cross of man and
           seahorse. The offspring of a flying marten. That's you
           Jasmin only you.

KARL: And only Tommi can see it. Only Tommi on his metal
           hunk of a lookout.

TOMMI: I'm waiting here leaning on this damn Mercedes in
           front of her window. Waiting for her to show up. To
           draw my blood into her emphysema. Stretch out my
           entrails with her snazzy boots. And make it wider
           inside me again. Make more room. For a breath of air.

KARL: When she got there it was almost three a.m.

TOMMI: She doesn't see me.

KARL: She doesn't see anything. And that has nothing to do
           with you.

TOMMI: She unlocks the front door.

KARL: You don't say a word.

TOMMI: Standing there in front of her house that night. She'd
           never been more beautiful than that.

KARL: You didn't come close enough to her.

TOMMI: In that moment she was closer to me than ever before.

KARL: Had you come closer. You would have smelled
           everything. The yeast in her breath. My sweat on her

skin. The flour in her red hair. But you. You just looked at her. And that was enough for you.

TOMMI: It made me happy somehow.

KARL: Night after night Tommi stood by her house. Later with dark clothes crouching behind darker cars.
And was happy. To just look at her.

TOMMI: Those were good times. Love. But with peace and quiet.

KARL: You call it peace and quiet. I call it terrorizing.

TOMMI: She didn't see me.

KARL: She saw you. She just thought. It's going to stop soon. The terror will be over soon.

TOMMI: I left her alone. In my own way.

KARL: And you left me alone too. No phone calls. Nothing. Meanwhile summer had come. I thought you knew everything. About Jasmin and me.

TOMMI: I didn't know a thing. You were my friend. You can't know that kind of thing without going crazy.
I just didn't feel like talking.

KARL: I missed you.

TOMMI: You kept fucking her in the bakery.

KARL: And you hit her in the park.

TOMMI: That happened in the heat of the moment. An accident.

KARL: After that she was always afraid.

11.

TOMMI: I went crazy lost my mind.

That's normal when someone tears your heart out.

KARL: Jasmin told me about what happened in the park.

TOMMI: It was a coincidence.
Suddenly she was walking in front of me.

KARL: With a guy.

TOMMI: The guy was strange. I thought so right away.
          Slender on top and kind of fat around the bottom.
          Hair down to his shoulders and greasy.
          I started throwing pebbles at them.

KARL: Then a bigger stone.
          It hit the guy in the back. He turned around.

TOMMI: Bright eyes almost turquoise. Shining out of his pimply
          face. Skinny arms no muscles nothing. He was a joke.
          I didn't even want to know his name.

KARL: The guy says. What the hell is your problem. And
          Tommi says. Hi.

TOMMI: Hi. To Jasmin not to him.

KARL: Get lost Tommi. Says Jasmin.

TOMMI: The guy says. Come on let's go. In a high voice.

KARL: Come on. To Jasmin not to him.

TOMMI: That was too much. That someone was talking to her
          like that. Come on. You're saying come on to her.

KARL: Jasmin says. Get lost Tommi. Leave us alone.

TOMMI: Alone. You two.

KARL: Tommi takes her by the arms. Takes the right one the
          left. He senses the fear in her muscles. This isn't what
          he wanted. To make her afraid. He just wanted her to
          himself again. All to himself. She says. I don't love you
          Tommi.

TOMMI: I don't love you. That just the way it is.

KARL: Tommi lets go of her.

TOMMI: Who do you love then. Him.

KARL: She laughs.

TOMMI: That's when it happened.

KARL: His eyes follow his own fist.

TOMMI: I couldn't help it. She laughed.

KARL: His fist hits her above the chin. Slides across her
          upper lip. To the side of her nose. And from the tip of
          her nose into the air. Her head falls back. Her balance

lost. Gravel under her cheek. Warmth spreading in her
nose. Flowing from inside to outside.

TOMMI: A nosebleed. Looked worse than it was.

KARL: Jasmin lifts her head. She talks to the guy. She says a
name.

TOMMI: She says. Phöbe.

KARL: The guy was a girl.

TOMMI: Right from the start I thought he was strange. But then
I just lost my mind.

KARL: Phöbe says. I'm calling the police.

TOMMI: Jasmin says. No.

KARL: Tommi leaves. At some point he starts running.

TOMMI: It wasn't what I wanted.

KARL: But it's what you did.

TOMMI: It was your fault. If it weren't for you none of this
would have happened.

KARL: It hadn't been the way you think for a long time.

TOMMI: You fucked my girlfriend. What more is there to think.

12.

KARL: It was the bakery. We rolled around on the laminate
floor on crumbs. We had bruises open wounds. On our
knees backs asses. Splinters from the kneading table
in our skin. We had flour in our pores sugar in our
breath. Once I stepped on the bread knife. The big one
with the wooden handle. The handle had the name
of the Greek woman on it. Helena. I started to bleed
between my toes.

And Jasmin took my foot in her mouth.
The air was always sweet. At some point heavy.
When I took her home with me.
To my room.
After three months.
Summer had arrived.
It was hot. But not heavy and not sweet either.

When I wanted to touch her.
In a regular old bed.
That's when she said. No.
And I didn't even try.
We missed the bakery.
Its air and the flour.
She used her puffer again for the first time.
I thought. When we see each other there again.
In the bakery.
Everything will be back to the way it was. Good.
As good as it can be anyway.
When you're losing your friend in the process.
When the time had come to go back to the bakery.
August had arrived. The eleventh.
The eve of our birthday.
Tommi's and mine.
Jasmin was with me.
We wanted to kiss each other touch each other.
We really tried.
But the sparks were gone.
The room had lost its magic.
Jasmin sneezed in my face.
We laughed and started baking a cake.
With three grams of hash in it just for you.
Tommi.
When we wanted to slice into it.
To taste a piece just after ten.
We couldn't find the big bread knife.

13.

TOMMI: I wanted to wait for Jasmin one last time.
In front of her house.
It was twenty past eleven.
In forty minutes it would be my birthday.
I wanted to give her the knife.
To tell her.
If I ever get too close to you again.
Slice my throat open with this knife.

I wanted to show her the spot. The place where you start.
Two centimetres below the ear.
That's what I wanted to tell her.
And then go see Karl.
For our birthday in the bakery.
Like every year.
Suddenly.
Out of the blue I missed you.

KARL: Jasmin got home at twenty to twelve. We hadn't touched each other. We'd baked a cake instead. A cake with a hole in the middle. A Guglhupf.

TOMMI: She noticed me right away.

KARL: Tommi was standing on the doorstep. She couldn't get past him. Tommi said he was sorry.

TOMMI: About what happened in the park. I'm sorry.

KARL: She stood in front of him. Absolutely calm. As if she had nothing to hide. A flowering tree sprinkling him with white flour with the whole bakery.

TOMMI: With the last four months of utter betrayal.

KARL: The vanilla kisses the anis-scented sweat. The rolling around in the flour. Our breath of cake and hash.

TOMMI: I could feel my heart. Pumping at first then racing. Into my throat my lungs my stomach. I was about to puke it out. My heart. Onto the street right in front of her feet. But I ran before that. To the bakery. To Karl.

KARL: The knife. He never gave it to her.

14.

TOMMI: When I got there Karl had already eaten two pieces of the cake.

KARL: It was twelve-thirty. I thought you weren't going to show.

TOMMI: We've celebrated all our birthdays in the bakery. Why wouldn't we this year.

KARL: I was so happy when you arrived.

TOMMI: You hugged me.

KARL: You didn't move.

TOMMI: Then you wished me happy birthday.

KARL: Happy birthday Tommi Bommi. Where the hell have you been.

TOMMI: Suddenly I found myself with a piece of cake in my hand.
           And you.
           What have you been up to.

KARL: Well. Baking. Lots of baking.
           Plaited loafs Danishes buns cinnamon rolls.
           My heart is flour my soul is dough.
           Tommi.
           I've missed you so much.

TOMMI: I dropped the cake.

KARL: You started rummaging around in your knapsack.
           I thought. Oh no. Not a present.
           I couldn't deal with a present.

TOMMI: I knew what you were thinking.
           Then I took the knife.
           And cut your throat.
           One cut.

KARL: Quick warm and precise.

TOMMI: Starting two centimetres below the right ear. Ending three millimetres above the left half of the collar bone.

KARL: My blood. An oval island dark and quiet around us.

TOMMI: Your eyes were closed.
           Your eyelashes calm.
           Your lips soft as if they'd just been kissed.
           Your arms touch my legs.
           Your left shoulder on the piece of cake.
           My shoes are black. Black Adidas.
           The blood level rises to the rubber soles and stays there.
           My feet stay dry.
           I knew. Once I leave here.

The radius of this island.
Nothing will be the way it used to be.

KARL: He takes off his shoes.
And walks into the room in his socks.
Five steps away from me.
To the cash register. He knows what to do with the day's takings.

TOMMI: Nothing but change.
I put all of it in his pockets.
It wasn't much.
A hundred and twenty Euros.
I fished the dripping shoes out of the blood.

KARL: Later he tells his father.
He didn't recognize me.

TOMMI: I just saw that someone was taking money from the cash. It was too dark to see. Karl was holding the knife. I twisted it out of his hand. I didn't recognise him. He was my friend. I killed him. I didn't mean to.

KARL: Later. When the police arrived. The forensic unit. The hearse. Later he cried. And puked on the sidewalk.

TOMMI: We were friends. Best friends. As they say.

KARL: The baker was shocked. He had trusted me. More than a son. Then he took Tommi in his arms.

TOMMI: And all that for of a hundred and twenty Euros.

KARL: Tommi was never accused of murder. Not by the law and not by his father either. What Jasmin thinks about this. We don't know. Maybe she doesn't care.

TOMMI: I think she went lesbian. When I saw her last. She was kissing a girl. In a kebab joint in the middle of June.

KARL: Two months after that in August Tommi would turn eighteen. And throw a garden party for his birthday.

III. Skin

Jule and Jasmin

1.

JASMIN: She's always there. She doesn't disappear. She's everything I've got. Everything I need. My oxygen my cortisone my life.

JULE: Don't forget to breathe, sweetie.

2.

JASMIN: Jule isn't the kind of person you chase after. Still. That's what I did.

JULE: You could hardly call that chasing could you.

JASMIN: Even her hair is a disaster. She cuts it herself with a pocket knife.

JULE: A lady's razor.

JASMIN: Some of it is shoulder-length. Some is cropped at the ear. On her left ear a scar.

JULE: Burnt. Not cut.

JASMIN: Her hair is tri-coloured. Dark on top lighter almost blond lower down. In between grey. Whole tufts of it. When I first met Jule. I imagined she was going to stink.

JULE: There are people who think worse things about me.

JASMIN: That she's not smart more on the stupid side.

JULE: Why else would you flunk out of school. Knowing it's after that that the real trouble starts.

JASMIN: Others find her aggressive. Her hair her stupidity her body. They think. Jule doesn't eat. Not enough. They think she went through tough times. Definitely. Just look at her.

JULE: They think other people don't have it easy either. And still they make something of themselves.
That shows optically and in other ways too.

JASMIN: They imagine she panhandles. At the main station or in front of the liquor store. Spare a Euro.

JULE: And where she sleeps. You don't even want to know.

JASMIN: Those are the mistakes people make.
With Jule.
Thinking she's the last person you'd chase after.

3.

JULE: My name is Jule.
I'm sixteen years old.
At fifteen I moved into a home for girls.
I know my way around that place like the back of my hand.
Twelve girls on each floor. One bathroom. Three shower stalls.
And one room with a bathtub. It locks.
That room is heaven and what's more.
I have a room to myself and a section of the fridge in the shared kitchen.
The girls are between fourteen and eighteen.
I haven't made any friends yet.
In two years I'll have to leave anyway.
Fixed relationships would only get in the way.
I'm doing fine.
Have a social worker all to myself twelve o'clock on Tuesdays.
If I don't feel like it that's fine too.
We're not your parents.
You have to understand that.
Got it.
Flunked out of school six months ago.
Your options are begging stealing turning tricks or getting a job.
There's a world of possibilities out there.
We'd be happy to help you find something.
I went for the infomercial thing.

The call centre job.
People interested in nativity sets ab toning systems knife sets.
I'm really enjoying it.
Being on the phone.
I've got it in my blood.
They noticed that about me right away.
They like me there.
At the call centre.
I wear a different blouse every day.

JASMIN: Batik blouses.
She's got them in all different colours.
The first one I got to see on her was red and blue.
She also has some in three colours.
Grey blue turquoise. Red yellow orange.
They're all god awful.
The last thing anyone would wear.
And underneath spotty skin.
Bruises scrapes open wounds.
At first I thought it was a rash.
Fungus scabies maybe something contagious.
Later I knew. It's from washing.

JULE: I wash myself three times a day.
Not in the bathroom.
In my own room over the sink.
I've got a job.
I can't afford to stink.

JASMIN: She washes herself with anything she can find.
Washcloths potholders scouring pads knife-tips fingernails.

JULE: I've got a peel. A double skin.
A few scrapes.
It's ornamentation. The preparatory work.
You've got to go deeper.
Where the white threads start to show.
That's where it flows. Where the juice is.
I'm not suicidal.
I'm an orange. I kiss the sun.
I hang on a golden tree.
I worship you. Life.

I'm well.
I'm back to normal again.
I'm on the up and up.
But who do you tell about it.
Unless maybe the whole world.
I'll keep saving up.
Then I'll buy some products.
Salves lotions enzymes. Nothing but the best.
And then I'll be a model.

JASMIN: She steals the soap from the bathroom at night.
Nivea Bebe CK Gucci Palmolive.
She smells different every day.
Always something new.

JULE: It was strongly suggested that I dress differently.
More appropriately.
Not as colourful not as baggy.

JASMIN: She's too skinny. Too skinny for her bones.

JULE: I weigh 101 pounds. Am five foot seven.

JASMIN: She eats. I've seen her eat.
I know she eats.
She breathes she laughs and she runs.
She's the fastest girl in town.
Her legs are long her kneecaps large her hips wide.
Her jeans cling directly to her bones.
None of her jeans find the skin on her bones.
But it's there.
Jule's skin is there.
Stretched over her bones.
A tent that makes no sense.
Taut over her broad shoulders.
The ganglion cyst on her wrist.
Her perfectly round scull.
A rage of bones covered with skin.
Veins and tendons branching out.
The promise of a landscape underneath it.
As blue and red and wild as her batik blouses.
I know what I'm talking about.
I've seen them and touched them too.
Her bones glow.
As if she's constantly running a fever.

But that's not what it is.
It's just the friction between skin and bones.
It's like how they started a fire in the stone-age.
I know what I'm talking about.
I've been through her skin and found her bones.
I know the way. Short and unusual.
It's all I need to know about Jule.
That she's a diamond beneath her clothes and her hair.

JULE: I wash my hair twice a day. Once a week I take the razor to my head.

JASMIN: She doesn't mean to be provocative with her knife technique.
She just likes the feeling.
On her scalp her neck behind her forehead.
When a metal blade connects hair root and brain.
When the root comes loose at some point.
One hair.
A single one.
Chosen.
Its colour always surprises her.

JULE: I had nothing to do with the colour.
Maybe I'm a calico cat.
They also have three colours.
And they're also more lucky than they are reasonable.
When I was eleven I put my ear on the stovetop.
I wanted to know if you can hear the warmth.
Now I know that scar tissue doesn't grow hair.

JASMIN: Jule is not stupid.
She's got more brains than all of you.
Nobody has grey hair at sixteen.
But she does.
Maybe that's why I ran after her.

JULE: You ran after me because I stole your cell phone. If you want to call it running.

4.

JASMIN: We're in the middle of a square.
The square in front of the Atlantik.

All around us diving board gymnasts café goers and
deceased
people.
I'm starting to write an SMS to Karl.
It happens to me in the middle of the day.
I like being sad.
You start imagining something and send an SMS into
the universe.
I miss you so bad.
Jule grabs the cell phone from my hand.
As if she wants to pull me out of this.
This swamp of sadness.

JULE: Whoa girl. I was just stealing it.

JASMIN: You thought I was too caught up in something. And
wanted to pull me out of it.

JULE: I didn't give a fuck what you were caught up in.
I'm not Jesus.
I was just stealing your cell phone.
Thought it would be fun.
Playing cops-and-robbers.
Running. A chase. Our hearts pounding.

JASMIN: Theft wasn't something that occurred to me.

5.

JULE: Our hands touched for a moment.
The phone connecting us.
Like in a relay race.
It felt good.

JASMIN: She looked at me for just a second. Or tried to anyway.

JULE: Looking into each others' eyes. I think it's overrated.

JASMIN: Jule's a bit cross-eyed.
Like I said not much just a little.
Her eyes are grey. And bright.
Her line of sight misses my pupils.
Off by maybe a millimetre.
It unsettles me. Strikes me in an unusual place.
Her light-grey glance knows a way directly underneath
my iris.

I swear.
Since then.
Since that first moment of eye contact.
I've felt a pressure under my eyelids.
The pressure comes from the inside.
From the other side of the skin.
I swear. It's her.
She's inside me.
And will always be.

JULE: Come with me.

JASMIN: What.

JULE: Come with me.

6.

JASMIN: She's running. My phone in her hand. She's
           zigzagging. As if she had trouble deciding.

JULE: What are you waiting for.

JASMIN: As if she wants to give me time.

JULE: Come with me.

JASMIN: She runs past the indoor pool. Swerves past a mother
           with a child. Jumps a beer bench in front of a café.
           She's wearing sandals. I'm wearing sneakers. Grey
           Nikes. When she reaches the kebab place that's when
           I set myself in motion.

JULE: That's really all you could call it.

JASMIN: Slowly at first. Then faster. As fast as I can. I can't go
           very fast. I've got emphysema you prickly witch. It's
           nothing. Nothing terrible. It's just that at fourteen I
           already had the lung volume of a forty-yearold woman.
           Now I'm sixteen. The woman is probably fifty. And I'm
           afraid you'll get away from me in these streets.

JULE: Hurry up.

JASMIN: She stops under the archways of the city trains. I could
           be wrong. But I think she's waiting.

JULE: It's no fun like this.

JASMIN: When I get within ten yards of her she starts running
again. Across the street. Straight into the organic
market. And I see her colourful back flashing between
the market stands. The blouse red blue comes sliding
off her shoulder. I catch a glimpse of the devastation
on her back. The blotches and her thin skin.
I get a cramp in my side.
Now.
My breath gets stuck between my ribs.
It can't move out. Is pinched in my organs.
I know the feeling.
And the fear. I know that too.
The fear always comes.
The fear that it'll stay there. My breath.
Because my lungs are bloated.
A baby's fat belly with no exit.
Because my fucking lungs cut my heart off.
Push it up into a corner.
Until it explodes with all its chambers.
And the last rush of blood spurts out of my pores lips
ears.
Because I ran too fast.
Put too much stress on my lungs.
Because some batik bitch stole my cell phone.
I want to yell.
But yelling only makes the feeling worse.
I wait.
To regain my breath.
And then my calm.
First the fear leaves me.
Then I see the batik of her blouse shining.
Slowly I cross the street.

JULE: Time to buy some flowers.

JASMIN: Jule is holding a gladiola in her hand.
Just one.
Its flowers are red and small.
I think. Flowers.
I think to myself. That'll calm the waters. Mine
included.
Suddenly I want to go to her.

Just like that.
She'll give me the gladiola.
I'll tell her my name.
I'm Jasmin.
I'm Jule.
We remember the cell phone only much later.
I put my hand to my head.
My hair is a red wilderness.
I want the dust of the short chase to show up on my face.
That would give us a reason to relax.
Jule takes money from her pocket.
The flower woman won't take it.

7.

JULE: How much is one.

JASMIN: The gladiolas aren't sold individually. Only in bunches of three or five.

JULE: But I just need one.

JASMIN: I'm sorry.

JULE: Then I'll pay for three. And just take one.

JASMIN: It doesn't work like that.

JULE: How does that not work.

JASMIN: It just doesn't work that way.

JULE: Take your hands off me.

8.

JASMIN: I put my hand on her arm.

The one without the flower.
No harm intended.
I only want to take her away.
Through the batik fabric I can feel the bone of her lower arm.
The bone feels hot.
Why don't you take the whole bunch.

JULE: You stay out of it.

JASMIN:	Suddenly her arm is gone. I try to find it but I can't. I swear. My fingers touch nothing but fabric. Red and blue. The fabric feels cool. Give me back my cell phone.
JULE:	Here. Take the damn flower.
JASMIN:	She hands the flower to the lady. My gladiola.
JULE:	Come with me.
JASMIN:	She says that to me. Come with me. And I know I'm not acting right around her. Not appropriately. Not the way I should act. Not at all. But come with me. That's a great sentence. It's all I want to hear. And I go with her.
JULE:	It just doesn't work that way.
JASMIN:	She runs back to the flower lady.
JULE:	Anything can work.
JASMIN:	She kicks the vase with the gladiolas three times with her sandals. With the third kick it falls over. Jule picks up a gladiola from the ground. Picks one at random. The flower lady doesn't say a word. The vase didn't break. When Jule is back with me she looks at me briefly. The gladiola in her hand. And I know it will always be a problem. Looking each other in the eyes with that slightly cross-eyed squint of hers. She starts running. Leaves me behind and runs to the park. I follow her. Walking very slowly. She didn't say it. Come with me.

But I've got the sentence inside me.
And I know she'll be waiting for me in the park.

9.

JULE: A hundred years later.

JASMIN: She is sitting on a bench.
Cross-legged.
The flower in her lap.
She looks at me as I come closer.
She hears my breath.
Give me my cell phone back.

JULE: Why don't you sit down.

JASMIN: Next to her the stem of the gladiola touches my leg.
It's cut at an angle.
It feels electric.
The touch is a sting.
I can feel it in my head below my skullcap.
Then I lose the connection to my feet.
I think. This is how poison works. This is what it feels like.
Good.
Jule takes my phone from her pocket.

JULE: I miss you so bad.

JASMIN: Give me that.

JULE: Who.

JASMIN: Who.

JULE: Yeah. Who. Who do you miss so bad.

JASMIN: Karl.

JULE: Karl.

JASMIN: My boyfriend.

JULE: Karl.

JASMIN: Give me that.

JULE: Do you guys fuck.

JASMIN: What.

JULE: Karl and you.
          Do you guys fuck.

JASMIN: Do we fuck.

JULE: That's what I'm asking.

JASMIN: I know I shouldn't laugh.
          I should remember his vanilla skin and his cinnamon
          breath.
          And then get sad.
          But it doesn't happen like that.
          It's too enjoyable. Talking with Jule.

JULE: So. What's he like.

JASMIN: Karl.

JULE: Yeah. Is he a good fuck.

JASMIN: Karl.

JULE: Yes.

JASMIN: Karl's dead.

10.

JULE: Really.

JASMIN: Really.

JULE: Crass.

JASMIN: We fucked.

JULE: Karl and you.

JASMIN: Yeah. In a bakery.
          Then he got stabbed.
          By his best friend.
          Tommi.
          I dated him too.

JULE: Sick.

JASMIN: She returns my cell phone. I could go now. Now there
          you have it. Now I'm sad. You don't believe me.

JULE: I don't give a shit.

JASMIN: She puts her head between her knees. I can see the
          scar on her ear. I want to touch her neck.

121

11.

JULE: Do you miss him.

JASMIN: No.

JULE: So it's not so bad then.

JASMIN: No.

JULE: You're writing your dead boyfriend an SMS. Even though you don't miss him at all.

JASMIN: Pretty sick right.

JULE: Pretty sick.

JASMIN: Her cheeks now have marks from the seams of her pants. And her lips. They're almost smiling.

JULE: There she is.

JASMIN: Who.

JULE: Natascha.

12.

JASMIN: She leaves. Leaves me. Walks through the park. With the flower. Walks over to a girl. I stay here. On the bench. What can I do. I'm a fifty-year-old woman. Jule doesn't say anything. She runs. Catches up with the girl. Jumps right in front of her.
           Jule's smile comes two minutes too late.
           The girl doesn't smile.
           Anyone would smile if Jule jumped in front of them holding a gladiola.
           But not the girl.
           The girl wants to keep walking.
           First Jule gives her money.
           Bills. Sticks them right into the pocket of her pants.
           The girl takes the money out again.
           Throws it down on the path.
           Next Jule gives her the gladiola.
           Jule starts to talk.
           With both hands free now.
           It's a real dance. A dance of her hands in the air.
           A monologue for a fish.

It looks beautiful.
And somewhat desperate.
The girl picks up the bills.
When they're done the girl gives the gladiola back to
Jule.

13.

JULE: So you're still here are you.

JASMIN: Who was that.

JULE: None of your business.

JASMIN: She gives me the gladiola.
          Puts it in my hand.
          The hand that had been open.
          It's been looking forward to the flower the whole time.
          I'm Jasmin.

JULE: Shitty name.

JASMIN: What's your name.

JULE: Are you tea or something.

JASMIN: She takes a cigarette out of her pocket.
          Unwrapped. Bent.
          Tobacco crumbles into her hand.
          She blows it into my face.
          Are you crazy.

JULE: I'm Jule.

JASMIN: If you smoke I have to go.

JULE: Then go.

JASMIN: She lights her cigarette.
          She smiles.
          Finally.
          The cigarette in her mouth.
          Her profile casual and beautiful. I take out my puffer.

JULE: What's that.

JASMIN: Cortisone.

JULE: Everything about you is so sick.

JASMIN: I pump the stuff into my lungs. I want to make her see
           what she's doing to me. Tobacco kills me.

JULE: So does cortisone.

JASMIN: I've got emphysema you know. Enzyme deficiency. My
           lungs get all bloated.
           I shouldn't even live in a big city.

JULE: Want a drag.

JASMIN: She holds the cigarette out for me.
           A cruel offer.
           Almost a kiss.
           I cough.
           So does she.
           To be funny.
           Then she pockets my puffer.
           Puts it where my cell phone used to be.
           Give it back.
           I need that.

JULE: What for.

JASMIN: To breathe you moron.

JULE: Oh you'll manage.

JASMIN: You're a real bitch Jule.

JULE: Where are you going.

JASMIN: I'm out of here.

JULE: You're nothing without your puffer.

JASMIN: You think there's only one of these in the world.

JULE: Why don't you stay a bit longer.
           Look. Smoke's gone air's clean.

JASMIN: Who was that. The girl.

JULE: Want to go for a walk. Real slow.

JASMIN: Screw you.

JULE: That was Natascha.

JASMIN: Pretty. Really pretty.

JULE: Pretty. Are you a lesbo or something.

JASMIN: Look who's the one who gave her the gladiola. You or
          me.

JULE: Who's the one holding the gladiola now. Her or you.

JASMIN: Not me.
          I lost it.
          It fell out of my hand.
          Fell underneath the bench.
          And that's where it stays.
          It glows there just as well.
          Then we take a little walk.

14.

JULE: Natascha can't hear. She only understands hands.

JASMIN: Have you been friends long.

JULE: She's not my friend.

JASMIN: Just forget it.

JULE: She's my sister.

JASMIN: Now she goes back.
          Searches for her cigarette in the grass.
          Looking back to me she smiles.
          The butt between her lips.
          And I know that I will never think her more beautiful
          than in this
          instant.
          With her smoke-smile. Standing five steps away from
          me.
          A distance that turns her skin into landscape.
          Colourful and wide.
          A kaleidoscope.
          The sun caught in a crystal.
          A distance that makes it seem impossible.
          To be surprised or disgusted or get infected with
          anything.
          A distance from which she comes shining towards me.
          With her spots and wounds.
          And I wish for nothing more than to be there.
          Where she is.
          To be in her skin.

No matter what that would mean.
Even if it meant that I'd scratch myself.
Bleed or kick the bucket.
The smoke won't light.
Do you cut yourself or something.

JULE: No. It's genetic.

JASMIN: Your sister doesn't show any sign of it.

JULE: She's lucky.

JASMIN: You two don't look alike.

JULE: We didn't grow up together.

JASMIN: And what about genetics and stuff.

JULE: Mind your own genetics.

JASMIN: I think your skin looks beautiful.
           Like sun caught in a crystal.

JULE: What.

JASMIN: Never mind.

JULE: So you don't believe that Natascha is my sister.
           You think I made her up. That's how sick you think I
           am.

JASMIN: I really couldn't care less.

JULE: Me neither. I'm broke. That bitch stole my money.

JASMIN: No she didn't.

JULE: Come on. You watched us.

JASMIN: You gave it to her.

JULE: I'm hungry.

JASMIN: And then. At the kebab place. I picked up the tab.
           And she told me about herself.
           About the doctors' questions.
           And how she met her sister.
           She eats meat with sauce and pita.
           And puts the lettuce aside.

15.

JULE: At the hospital.
A year ago.
I tried something. In the bathtub at the girls' home.
Involving sleeping pills.
Not many. Just twelve.
It wasn't that I wanted to die
It was just a breathing experiment.
I wanted to know what it's like.
To fall asleep under water.
When everything fills up with water.
Every hole orifice. Every pore.
Every tube of your entrails. The lungs too.
I was interested in what it's like.
When you wake up.
If you bloat up or explode in the end.
Or if your skin opens up somewhere.
If it's possible.
To create new air passages.
That's what I was wondering.
If you can turn into a fish in your sleep.
Become a gill-breather overnight.
But they broke the door open.
The door to the room with the bathtub.
Those social worker bum-fucks.
Fished my naked body out of the water.
And I had only just fallen asleep.
In the hospital they opened up the ol' locks.
Made all that bubble bath flow out again.
Those destroyers of fish.
Pumped me up with air.
So much for my gills.
Only my sleep. It was super-humanly long.
Seventeen hours.
And then the questions.
Can you hear me.
Your name.
Can you tell us your name.
How old are you.
Where do you live.
Can you describe the way home for us.

127

Do you know what you did.
Fucking memory fanatics.
Oxygen fascists.
Where do the wounds the scratches come from.
What happened with your ear.
Do you injure yourself.
How long has this been going on.
Do you want us to contact someone.
Friends. Relatives. Your parents.
Can you tell us how much you weigh right now.
Do you find your appearance aggressive.
Would you call yourself aggressive.
Are you willing to accept help.
Can you open yourself to another person.
Does physical closeness make you uncomfortable.
I answered all the questions.
Then asked to be left alone.

And found my sister.
We were sharing a room.
Three weeks together in the psychiatric ward.
She didn't say a word.
Not to the doctors. Not to visitors.
The tag at the foot of her bed said her name was
Natascha.
She would sometimes give me a smile.
And I was so grateful.
For her silence.
Aren't you hungry.

16.

JASMIN: I'm vegetarian.

JULE: You have no appreciation for the beauty of the world.

JASMIN: I think you're incredibly beautiful.

JULE: No lover of beauty is vegetarian.
    Just look at that. The kebab man with his kebab beast.
    Ten-thousand slivers from a hog's ass-cheek.
    It's refined. Now that's what I call art.

What are you staring at.
Look at him. Not at me.

JASMIN: We can do that too. Be silent.

JULE: If you touch me I'm out of here.

JASMIN: If I touch her she'll disappear.
I know what I'm talking about.
I already lost the bone of her lower arm once.
I inhale everything.
The garlic from her pores.
The meat on the rotating spit.
The grease in the air.
I've never had more room inside of me.

JULE: I knew you were a lesbo.

JASMIN: What about Karl.

JULE: Karl is dead.
The dead don't fuck.
If you don't fuck you're not a couple.

JASMIN: I need to get out of here.

JULE: Why.

JASMIN: I can't breathe anymore.

JULE: Do you want me to kiss you.
Give you air.

JASMIN: Stop looking at me like that.

JULE: Why.

JASMIN: You're cross-eyed.

JULE: I'd like to touch you.

JASMIN: Really.

JULE: But you can't touch me.

JASMIN: Because then you'd disappear.

JULE: Exactly.

JASMIN: Android-bullshit.

JULE: I find you incredibly beautiful too.

17.

JASMIN: What are those.

JULE: Toothpicks.

JASMIN: So many.

JULE: We have to explore some possibilities.

JASMIN: She's always. Always on the lookout for possibilities.
            She doesn't want to disappear.
            She's just looking for another place.
            It's not the same thing.
            She believes in it. Believes that it exists.
            The world behind the skin.
            Beneath the orange-planet.
            Where pleasure and pain are siblings.
            Where life is not a fifty-year-old woman.
            Where we're swept away.
            She believes in it. In the possibility.
            I bow to that.
            This trust.
            Stop it.

JULE: No.

JASMIN: The first toothpick in the palm of her hand.
            About 2 centimetres deep.
            The second in the centre of the hand.
            Where two lines cross.
            The third just below the pinkie.
            Even deeper than the first one.
            The fourth just below the wrist.
            I watch.
            And her hand turns pink. It looks healthy. Almost
            beautiful.
            Shots of light in my body.
            No connection no pain. Only shots.
            The sole of my foot vertebra coccyx.
            The last one hits me behind the forehead.
            My mouth is open.
            But I'm not yelling.
            Pull them out.

JULE: You pull them out.

JASMIN: One two three four.
           I'm a bright room. A feast of light inside me.
           Then comes the blood.
           Flows in all directions. Dark. Fast.
           Over the middle of her hand and over the lines of her
           palm.
           Between her fingers and underneath her nails.
           Flowing further. From her palm to her colourful blouse-
           sleeve.
           I hold her hand.
           It doesn't disappear.
           It's warm and light.
           Droplets fall onto the lettuce on her plate.
           I close my eyes.
           I cry with closed eyelids.
           Can't tell the difference anymore between salt blood
           and light.

JULE: Are you afraid.

JASMIN: No.

JULE: I bit my tongue.

18.

JASMIN: The inside of her mouth glistens.
           I can hear her swallow. She swallows blood.
           Our hands grasping tightly.
           I hear her scream.
           I inhale it her scream.
           Her lip bursts between mine.
           Her jaw in my gums.
           My eyelashes against one of her temples.
           The silence around us.
           The kebab man clears the table underneath our touch.
           He's not surprised.
           Two girls kissing after a good kebab.
           He's seen worse.
           He didn't hear Jule's scream.
           It's inside me.
           Races through my body. Opens my pores.

Takes everything from me. My fear too.
I feel her hand. Always. Even now I feel it.
The warmth and the desire to run.

IV. Ears

ALBERT and NATASCHA

1.

NATASCHA: First I listened to your feet.
Underwater at the Atlantik.
The waves of your big toes.
Between them chlorine bubbles.
A foot concert.
Your pink soles are singing a song for me.
Soft and beautiful.
I can hear the hairs in my ears dancing.

ALBERT: Pink soles.
I had heard this about you.
About how difficult it is. To have a normal conversation
with you.

NATASCHA: I was surprised too.
Surprised at your underwater song.
Because otherwise nothing but garbage comes out of
you.

ALBERT: That you're impolite.
I had heard that too.
When others are speaking. You make noises.
Sometimes.
That's what I heard.
Sometimes they say you gargle with your spit.
In the middle of a conversation.
And then there's your humming.
The way grandmas hum.

NATASCHA: Mmmmmmmmmmm.

ALBERT: That about sums it up.

2.

NATASCHA: Scraping with your feet scratching fabric.
Upholstery pants skin. Sometimes your ear.
Breathing. Loud. Through the mouth.

Clicking your tongue. Swallowing spit even if there's nothing to
swallow.
Humming.
Mmmmmmmmmmmmm.
M.
A resonating body a beehive.
This letter is a gift of the heavens.
In your ears your membranes.
In the little hairs on your skin.

And you forget everything. The fear too.
Fear of someone starting a conversation.
His voice is directed at me.
Voices kick holes in my skull.
Tear down walls in my brain.
Bring everything to a grinding halt. Any thought any
idea.
I can't listen.
I haven't got it in me.
A conversation.
Is nothing but pain for me.
Voices.
Loud soft deep bright shrill.
Children's voices teachers' voices mothers' voices.
Friends strangers pop stars.
TV voices radio voices subway announcements.
I try to not hear them.
Then to overpower them.
I stick paper balls in my ears.
People have stopped taking offence.
We've made an arrangement.
They have given up on me.
The heaven of silence.
Teachers bury their hope.
Students stay out of my way.
My mother took me to a psychiatric clinic.
She thought in there I might find my voice again.
The desire to talk.

The crazy girl in my room thought I was her sister.
No sense of hearing. And socially a lost cause.
I still see her sometimes.
She gives me money and talks with her hands.
I don't need that.
I'm not deaf or poor.
I'm doing fine just look at me.
I don't blather on and flap my jaw at everyone.
I'm a friend to the world.
A pleasant contemporary.
I'm not looking for quiet. I'm looking for music.
For melodies beyond the chatter.
Stretches of highway stones to trip over bats of eyelashes.
Skin hitting against skin.
Knocking on the walls of your skull. Worms in the wood.
Sneezing coughing taking in breath.
Water inside me. Sea water drinking water chlorine water.
I love the zoo.
Monkeys shrieking hippos farting wings fluttering.
I could be an animal among animals.
A bear an ant a penguin.
I'm a goldfish.
Until a gull comes along.
Tucks me into her beak and carries me far far away.
Albert.

ALBERT: Shit. Ten past six.

NATASCHA: Student hour at the Atlantik is over.

ALBERT: Which means paying extra.
Two Euros that is.
I've got nothing on me. Not a cent.

NATASCHA: That Albert is able to fly was a surprise to me.
The first time was at the side of the pool.
When he stood in front of me on one leg.

Like a budgie about to go to sleep.
At that point I still thought I might be imagining it.

3.

ALBERT: The thing I do with my leg is a nervous tic.
A nervous habit. A kind of ritual to calm myself.
Others whistle or pinch themselves.
I lift my leg up.
It's got nothing to do with flying.
No idea how it happened.
How we stayed past student hour.

NATASCHA: Albert.

ALBERT: The moment Natasha says my name I forget
everything around me
for a second.
The time the money the leg.

NATASCHA: That's when I see it.
Just briefly just slightly above the tiled floor.
But I can see that he's hovering in the air.

ALBERT: Shit.

NATASCHA: I know it's just him.
Albert.
Who shits his purple swim-trunks over two Euros.
Even though he could be swimming in money.
A cabin by the sea.
Where others go swimming he's at home.
Bourgeois kid preppy keener blatherer.
Self-important snob in a corduroy jacket.
When he gives presentations he puts on red-rimmed
glasses.
He's someone who always has a presentation to give.
On emperor what's-his-face the eighth.
Chromosome research stochastic studies periodic
tables.
Last year he was elected student representative.
In the afternoon he coaches the girls' volleyball team.
Someone like him would do anything.
He's in the chess club. Acts in the drama club.
Started the West-Africa Outreach Group.

Someone like him gets involved. In everything.
Always has something to say.
He's no riddle to me no mystery.
He's sheer terror.

ALBERT: Shit.

NATASCHA: I don't know where it comes from.
The music inside me.
He says. Shit.
A shrieking shrill sound.
I've heard that sound coming from llamas drinking water.
But I know it's impossible.
I know it's just him.

ALBERT: Outreach.
King of the Keeners.
There is something though. In his voice.
That turns beneath my skull.
And scratches.
Beautiful. Not painful.
A needle on vinyl.
Music. Not garbage.
I know who you are.
Albert.
The most unlikely of human beings in my system.
The most abnormal of all encounters.
The worst conversation possible.
I know my head should be bursting.
Even just thinking about a conversation.
He's hovering just above the floor.
I don't have to look at this.
I don't have to say anything.
So far we've never said a word to each other.
Cramp.

ALBERT: What.

NATASCHA: In your foot.

ALBERT: Oh. No. Do you have one.

NATASCHA: Me. No. My feet are fine.

4.

ALBERT: Natascha. Wow. Natascha.

5.

NATASCHA: Natascha. Natascha.
           A miserable word.
           That's how it always starts.
           Natascha.
           After that nothing but night. Nothing.
           That's what it's like my name.
           A cruel beginning.
           Three torturous syllables.
           Three As. Three yelps of pain.
           A T in the middle.
           A beat a trembling t-t-t-t-t.
           A pulsing in the auricle. A tensing in the brain
           muscles.
           What follows I know it it's always the same always
           pain.
           Words words words.
           Questions little jokes words words.
           What follows. I never understand it. Never.
           A voice shoots into me.
           Bursts my eardrum.
           Shoots letters into my small head.
           Tears down bridges between my organs.
           Pressure on the eyes velvet on the tongue shortness of
           breath.
           My brain bursts into flame my lips twitch.
           Someone wants to talk to me wants to hear answers.
           It often starts with my name.
           I say nothing. I can't
           It's not that don't have an answer. I don't have a voice.
           My answer is a scream.
           Nobody hears it. I don't scream audibly.
           I want to leave. As fast as I can.
           I don't run.
           I can't find the bridge to my legs.
           I'm gushing in bloodstreams scream in soundproof
           chambers.

Then I smile.
When someone says my name I smile.
When everything inside me turns to night my face smiles.
My smile is a free spirit.
I know it's strange.
Smiling doesn't fulfil the expectations doesn't count as an answer.
Smiling is always too little. Or too much.

ALBERT: Natascha.

NATASCHA: When

ALBERT: says my name there's no smile in me. Only music.
I know who he is.
Student rep Albert. Hero of class contributors.
But the sound of his voice has the power to carry me.
With three syllables across the kiddy pool.
I'm afraid.
It's a new fear.
I'm afraid he might go without saying another word.

ALBERT: We'll have to pay extra.

NATASCHA: Don't shit your pants over it Albert.

6.

ALBERT: I know her name.
Natascha.
Otherwise I don't know her.
We go to the same school but that doesn't mean anything.
Two years ago we were in the same grade.
Nine B.
Then she had to repeat a grade and after that she repeated another
one because she felt like it.
Now I'm in grade eleven. She's in nine A.
It doesn't matter to me.
But if I were her I'd find it strange.
Extremely strange.
She's strange.
She's wild.

She claps her hands totally out of the blue.
Then she rubs them against her temples.
Last year she was in a clinic. Psychiatric ward. Three weeks.
After that she was exactly the same.
Strange as always.
She doesn't talk. Especially not to me.
When we see each other at school we're like people in the street.
We don't look up. Don't say a word.
I don't know what kind of world she lives in.
And don't care.
I've got enough on my plate as it is.
Her hair is light brown her eyes are light brown.
She's a clearing in the woods a feast for the eyes.
Absolutely the most beautiful girl in school.
I'm really surprised that she knows my name.

NATASCHA: I can lend you some.

ALBERT: Really.

NATASCHA: Twenty minutes. By the turnstile.

7.

ALBERT: She's late.
Whatever.
Time doesn't matter now.
We'll have to pay extra anyway.
Natascha. Through grade nine three times.
A little dim. A humming grandma.
I've got rehearsal tomorrow after school.
No. It's the weekend.
Five to seven and I'm a little confused.
Too much chlorine no money.
Today is Friday.
If she doesn't show up I'll say I'll pay tomorrow.
They know me here.
That should be okay.
If she doesn't show I'll have her paged.
Little
Albert is waiting for the beautiful Natascha at the

turnstile.
But she'll come.
No. Not the foot. Not now.
My left foot goes up.
Piss. That's what I should have done.
Talking is always nicer.
When you don't have to piss.
Never mind.
She wouldn't start a conversation anyway.
Maybe she's left already.
I have to make those Goethe photocopies. Werther.
There is something under my feet. A feeling.
Not a touch. More like feeling someone's gaze.
As if being looked at from below.
Then comes the hovering.
Right in front of the turnstile.
Is this flying now or something.
From the point of view of physics it's surprising.
I'm waiting for Natascha.
And have no idea why it's happening.
I'll think about it later. Later.
Just normalise for now. Gain some solid ground.
There she is.
Her hair dry. She's looking serious and beautiful.
As if she wanted to say something.
She doesn't.
Holding the change in her hand.
I go over to her.
It's a strange sensation.
It's taking a step down without there being a step.

NATASCHA: Are you drunk or something.

ALBERT: Can we meet at school tomorrow. For the money.

NATASCHA: Well it's the weekend tomorrow.
But sure. If you want to.
We can climb the fence.

ALBERT: I mean Monday.

NATASCHA: Two days from tomorrow.

ALBERT: Yes.

NATASCHA: Alright.

ALBERT: I ran all the way to the subway.

8.

NATASCHA: I went to school on Monday holding my head high.
But Albert. Albert didn't show up.

ALBERT: I completely forgot something. I was all mixed up on
Friday at the Atlantik.

NATASCHA: I'm in front of his classroom.
Eleven B.
As if I'm still one of them.
Nobody's talking to me.
Nobody's acting like we used to be in the same grade.
Albert hasn't shown up.

ALBERT: No idea how that could have happened.

NATASCHA: I've been waiting. Seven minutes.
Someone like him would never be later than seven
minutes.
Then comes the quiet of the hall. Empty not nice.
I go back. Back to my generation.
Now my classmates are all two years younger than
me.
Algebra.
I roll some paper balls.
Get called to the chalkboard.
Because I'm late and anyway.
The chalk splinters.
A screeching sound where my fingers press.
A giant coordinate plane.
Not bad really not so bad and that's how far I get. A
Somebody throws a paper ball to the front. A
Somebody laughs. A
The paper ball hits the x-axis. A
I run out I'm quick like never before. A
The bang of the closing door doesn't reach my ears. A
I'm headed for the bathroom. A
To empty myself into a bowl with a roar. A
Getting there is crashing from one wall to the other. A
Am I trashed or something. A
Stop. A

Take your time. A
You're not feeling sick. A
There's nothing inside you that could come up. A
Stay here. A
Lift a leg. A
I'm a budgie. A
Tears. A
Do budgies cry. A
In any case I pee through my pants onto the light-grey
laminate floor. A
At home there's a letter waiting for me.

9.

ALBERT: Saturday. November 17th.
Hi Natascha.
I'm sorry I can't give you the money on Monday.
Because I forgot about the chess tournament.
(Even though I've been looking forward to it for
months.
It's the best of the best of all sixteen to eighteen year
olds.
And it's all happening in the beautiful and wild Black
Forest.)
I have no idea where my mind went.
"I know not whether it is day or night; the whole world
is nothing to
me."1
(Goethe. The Sorrows of Young Werther. Letter of June
19th.)
I'll be home Tuesday night.
1 Translated by Sir Walter Scott, 1772
Suggestion. Let's do our little transaction on
Wednesday after school in the cafeteria. Around two-
thirty. The drama club people will be there too for their
copies. The copies of Werther. By the way. I've got
the role of Werther. Not Albert. That means learning
all those lines. All those letters he writes. Maybe you
could make it on Wednesday. Adieu. Albert.

NATASCHA: A fir tree as the letterhead. Some youth hostel's logo.

ALBERT: Hi Natascha. God.

NATASCHA: His voice is racing through my head. His handwriting slapping against my eyelids.

ALBERT: Adieu.

NATASCHA: I don't know what's going on. Werther June transaction. I don't know why you would look forward. to the Black Forest. I also don't know whether it's day or night. I don't give a fuck. I just pissed on the floor at school. Hi Natascha. Wednesday two-thirty. I read the letter again from the top.

10.

ALBERT: On Wednesday an absolute writhing. In bed in the shower in the subway. Hi Natascha. I can't believe it. A letter. Nobody writes letters. By the way. I've got the role of Werther. Not Albert. Shit. I'll give her the money and that'll be that. Adieu. Albert. It is what it is. It's nothing. Just a letter. A letter. From the beautiful and wild Black Forest. At two-thirty it'll all be over. Two Euros. Forget about it. Clear your head. We'll finish the deal.

The student rep election is coming up on Friday.

11.

NATASCHA: Wednesday morning I'm running a temperature.
It's going up.
At seven it's already at thirty-nine.
At seven-thirty diarrhoea.
Limbs like cello strings dark sweet pain.
Pressure in the ears then occlusion.
A good start.
Fever total evacuation of the bowels drowsiness.
The perfect excuse.
Floating through the day.
Anaemic soundless.
Nice to wake up like this.
Usually. But not today.
Please not today.
Today is Wednesday and I have to be in the cafeteria at two-thirty.
The cafeteria.

Chatter-hell.
Cushioned chamber of the princely couples.
A room in the basement. Hidden sealed off.
To me a natural taboo.

ALBERT: When she enters the room I lose everything.
Shyness the writhing the letter.
The copies of Werther slide out of my hands.
The expression on my face. That I wanted to dedicate
to her.
Rather busy a little surprised.
I lose that too.
Her eyes hit my lower arm.
My arm jerks away.
It's a bad start.
Nothing's going as planned.
Her throat is red.

NATASCHA: A red sweater.
My best colour for this trip to the basement.
What can I say.
My cheeks are glowing.
My forehead is throwing sparks.
In my ears the dark plucking on the strings of my
limbs.
He's alone.
All alone.
I really should have stayed in bed.

ALBERT: Warmth enters the room with her.
I want to say something. I can't.
My lips are dry. So are hers.
I want to get up. I stay in my chair.
She looks at my feet.

NATASCHA: They're both suspended in the air.

ALBERT: It doesn't show so much when I'm sitting down.

NATASCHA: My ears release the pressure.
A new years' blast.
Blood is bubbling.
Two drops are on the floor.
The floor is red.
It doesn't show very much.

ALBERT: Her breath comes streaming hot into the room.

NATASCHA: The lenses of his glasses fog up.

ALBERT: The glasses. That was just an idea. Worn purposely
              but a mistake.

NATASCHA: Really too bad Mr. Penguin. Now I can't see your eyes.

ALBERT: I thought. Glasses.
              They make you look smart and also a little distant.
              The glasses would make up for the stunt with the
              letter.
              With glasses you're someone who always
              communicates through
              letters.
              Someone who's sick of making phone calls.
              Who prefers the written word.
              I thought. She might like that.
              I didn't factor in the heat.
              Hi Natasha.
              Are you not feeling well.
              Do you have a fever.
              Why don't you sit down.

NATASCHA: I had imagined it differently.
              A cafeteria like this.
              I imagined a basement mined with voices.
              A line of fire of ice cold glances.
              I didn't think he'd be sitting here alone in this heat.
              It's a desert dream not a cafeteria.
              And I'm a sand flea.
              Ready for a little chat.
              So. How was your thing.
              Did you win.

ALBERT: What.

NATASCHA: The chess thing.

ALBERT: Oh that. No.

NATASCHA: Because of the Black Forest. Too beautiful and too
              wild.

ALBERT: I was in a completely different place.

NATASCHA: So you weren't in the Black Forest.

ALBERT: In my mind.

12.

NATASCHA: It's all very easy.
We're spitting flea silk into the desert air.
The retard and the student rep.
The most ridiculous of all combinations.
The blackest of visions.
The last possible conversation.
Now it's music.
Finally he takes off his glasses.

ALBERT: Her face is white.
Her eyes are shining.
They're blinding me.
I don't know what it is.
Her backlight or my defective vision.
When she starts talking my temperature goes up.

NATASCHA: Is it always this quiet down here.

ALBERT: Here. No. Never.

NATASCHA: This is the first time I've been here.

ALBERT: Okay.

NATASCHA: It's actually nice.

13.

ALBERT: I'm not kidding myself.
This conversation hasn't happened.
I know it's a dream.
Let's stick to the facts.
She's running a fever.
Maybe I caught it from her.
Why doesn't she stay in bed when she's sick.
She is different from me. Very different.
She is going to fail school.
She doesn't say a word about my glasses.
Not a word about my letter.
She's not human.
She's the most beautiful girl at school.

Touching her.
Touching her would be like bursting through the clouds.
Too beautiful to be true.
Then she'd be gone.
Or I'd wake up.
That'd be good.
If she disappeared I'd have a clear head again.

NATASCHA: What are you thinking.

ALBERT: Next Friday is the student rep election.

NATASCHA: Then he sneezes.

ALBERT: She's still here.

14.

NATASCHA: I look at him.
His sneezing makes the corner of my mouth itch.
I want to throw his glasses to the floor.
Hear the glass clink.
Flutter through his eyelashes with my lips.
Bang against his teeth with my teeth.
I feel like touching his hair.
I want to know if it's soft or if it rustles.
Wonder if he'll yell when I tear at it.
Or only whisper.
Suddenly I find everything about him interesting.

ALBERT: That's when the door to the cafeteria opens.

14.

NATASCHA: First Laurent comes in. The guy from Africa. With hair yellow as egg yolk.

ALBERT: He's here about the petition. Fundraising for victims of the rebels.

NATASCHA: Why is he coming just now. At two thirty.

ALBERT: Because I asked him to.
Wednesday at two thirty.
Because I thought it would impress her.

That I know a guy from the Cape Verde Islands and
am concerned
about the issues of his home country.

NATASCHA: Their voices roll through my head. My head turns cold.

ALBERT: Hi Laurent.

NATASCHA: Damn hot in here.

ALBERT: Are you here about the petition.

NATASCHA: No. I'm here for a coffee.

ALBERT: This is **NATASCHA:** by the way.

NATASCHA: Here's all your shit.

ALBERT: Natascha. This is Laurent. From Togo. Cape Verde
Islands.

NATASCHA: Listen King Keener. I'm from here. My hair is blond my
soul too. Shove your petition up your equator. And it's
Fogo. Okay. Fogo. Not Togo.

ALBERT: Fogo.

NATASCHA: Mmmmmmmmmmmm.

16.

ALBERT: I can hear her. She's humming. I like it. Her humming.
It carries him away. Laurent. To Fogo or Togo or just up
to the first floor. The door opens.

NATASCHA: And now on to sports.

17.

ALBERT: Phöbe from the volleyball team.

NATASCHA: I've got to tell you something.

ALBERT: Practice is going to happen later this Friday. Four
o'clock.

NATASCHA: I'm not going.

ALBERT: The student rep election is at two.
I got nominated again.

NATASCHA: I don't think I can make it.

ALBERT: Were you nominated too.

NATASCHA: To practice.

ALBERT: To volleyball.

NATASCHA: Yeah. No big deal.

ALBERT: But we've got a game on Saturday.

NATASCHA: Well I'm in love.

ALBERT: That has nothing to do with it. Absolutely nothing.

NATASCHA: Yes it does.

ALBERT: No it doesn't.

NATASCHA: Isn't this NATASCHA

ALBERT: What.

NATASCHA: What's wrong with her.

ALBERT: What.

NATASCHA: What's she humming for.

ALBERT: She's not humming.

NATASCHA: What's she smiling for.

18.

ALBERT: She's perfectly quiet. Has stopped humming. She's
             sitting here. Here with me. Smiling. I won't be fooled.
             She's smiling and I know things are going downhill.
             With her smile the room temperature goes down. I
             can feel the table underneath my hands. It's moving.
             I know it's inside her. The noise. Her humming. She's
             transmitting it. Via the table legs the table top into
             my hands. I want to move my arm. It's fallen asleep.
             Numb on the outside inside a hissing. When the three
             Werther people show up. I barely have an ear for
             them.

19.

NATASCHA: Albert / Man we're late / And you're waiting here / At
             least you're not alone / Hi Natascha / Hello / It's me
             Sandy. We used to be in the same grade. Klaus too /

Hi / She's somewhere else / What's going on. / Klaus isn't your mother's job something to do with nerves / It's freezing in here / It's called neurology / Are those the copies / We actually wanted to talk a bit about the casting / Werner just read the last letter to us again / Sandy said why don't I try it. Just to see / I just wanted to know what it sounds like in Werner's voice not yours / I said that really wouldn't be cool. Without asking you and stuff / I think. And so does Klaus / I'll stay out of this / Of course. Klaus always stays out of stuff / So if you really want to be Werther that's alright with us. It's just / It would be kind of funny if Albert plays Albert and Werner Werther / But I somehow think it'd be better / Me too actually / In a way it's not fair. Albert already put so much into it. Made the copies and everything / Albert is a good role too / Albert / Aren't you going to say anything.

20.

ALBERT: Silence.

NATASCHA: He says nothing.

ALBERT: She closes her eyes.

NATASCHA: Something snaps.

ALBERT: A scream.

NATASCHA: It tears itself free. From the soil into the light. It's all I've got. My bones my blood my heart. When it's out I'm a thing of the past. Albert takes my hand. We're all by ourselves.

ALBERT: Where they went. The others. With their things. Werther volleyball West Africa. I don't know. Maybe we're here and they're not. Or the other way around. Doesn't matter. We're all by ourselves.

NATASCHA: My body is getting lighter. I have no strength in my neck.

ALBERT: A string of blood. From her ear to her throat. As if her sweater were hanging from an earring.

NATASCHA: Probably I drop to the floor.

ALBERT: She falls off her chair.

NATASCHA: I'm alright.

ALBERT: I don't know what to do.

NATASCHA: He kisses me.

ALBERT: Since the floor's gone anyway.

21.

NATASCHA: Are you kissing me because the screaming is irritating
             you.

ALBERT: No.

NATASCHA: It's actually really nice. The silence.

ALBERT: Pretty nice.

NATASCHA: Do you think I'm dead.

ALBERT: You're not dead.

NATASCHA: Well that'd be pretty fucking macabre.
             Kissing me.

ALBERT: You're not dead.

NATASCHA: Thank God you're not wearing your glasses.

ALBERT: Thank God.

NATASCHA: Glasses just kind of get in the way of kissing.

ALBERT: And of flying.

NATASCHA: Is this flying or something.

ALBERT: There is nothing closer to flying than this.

NATASCHA: Albert. Albert. I was so completely wrong about you.
             I thought. Talking to you. Would be a nightmare.

ALBERT: I also thought it couldn't happen.

NATASCHA: What's that jingling sound.

ALBERT: The two Euros.

NATASCHA: Am I dead.

ALBERT: Well how do you feel.

NATASCHA: Now.

ALBERT: Yeah.

NATASCHA: I feel fantastic.

V. Tongue

BEATE and LAURENT

1.

BEATE: We were together for seven weeks. Went to the movies five times. Out for a drink eight times. Stayed overnight at each other's place four times. Never had sex. Once he cut my hair. We ate together three times.

LAURENT: Twice a kebab. And we shared a pizza.

BEATE: After seven weeks he says he wants to cook for me. Just like that an invitation of sorts.

LAURENT: Next Saturday your place.

BEATE: My place. It's pretty empty at my place at the moment. My parents have been off on their ski vacation for a few days already. Far away where there's snow even in the fall. He knew full well that's where they were.

LAURENT: All of a sudden she thought I might be dangerous. Attack her. Like an animal or a pygmy.

BEATE: It's not unheard of. There are movies about it books thousands of examples.

LAURENT: Saturday six o'clock.

BEATE: Alright.

LAURENT: Your stove my ingredients.

BEATE: Is that some kind of joke.

2.

LAURENT: When I arrive at her place. Saturday at five to six. She's already smoked two joints by the open window.

BEATE: I did it for you. It subdues anxiety and stimulates the appetite.

LAURENT: I did this for you too. Dragging all this stuff across the courtyard and up to your apartment.

BEATE: From above I saw his yellow kinky-haired head. On his back a white duffel bag. In his right hand a black travel bag. In his left a pink bag. Suddenly I was filled with longing and joy. As if he were coming home from a long journey.

LAURENT: Of course I knew her parents were on a ski vacation.

BEATE: The kiss at the door. As if we are strangers.

LAURENT: I should have put my luggage down first.

BEATE: That's not it. It's the taste.

LAURENT: Lemon and coriander. I did some of the cooking ahead of time. Taste-tested.

BEATE: It's not that.

3.

LAURENT: She takes the pink bag from my hand.

BEATE: My lips are burning. Something's written on the bag in yellow letters.

LAURENT: True Love Tapioka.

BEATE: And now I know. I was wrong. Tonight will remain unequalled. I know there will never be another supper like this. None that will compare.

4.

LAURENT: This needs to go in the fridge.

BEATE: Pudding.

LAURENT: Corn pudding.

BEATE: Corn. Right.
Are you sure.

LAURENT: It takes four hours to set.

BEATE: Four hours.

LAURENT: For us that's way too short.

5.

BEATE: He turns on the oven.
Takes a casserole dish out of the black travel bag.
A black square. Silver at the top.
Amazing. Casserole.

LAURENT: For the entrée.

BEATE: He removes the aluminium foil from the casserole dish.
The casserole is white. Powdered sugar. Almonds.
Brown lines tracing letters.
What is this.

LAURENT: Cinnamon.

BEATE: What does it mean.

LAURENT: B and L.

6.

BEATE: Beate and Laurent.
It's not a fairy tale. Even if it started like that.
More than seven weeks ago.
At dusk.
In the silver hour in which you see a veiled world
through the lattice of
your lashes.
The music is electronic.
The grass kisses your feet.
And you smile at the world after your third joint.
It all started with a garden party.
A little boredom.
And a blond guy falling out of the hedge.

7.

LAURENT: The casserole will take forty minutes.

BEATE: What are we drinking.
Beer coke water.

LAURENT: Wine.

BEATE: Wine.

LAURENT: I brought red wine.

BEATE: Wine isn't really my thing.

LAURENT: Tasting it makes her cough.
             The second sip goes down easier.

BEATE: What the hell is this stuff.

LAURENT: Wine from Fogo.

BEATE: Tastes like smoke.

LAURENT: That's because of where the grapes are grown.

BEATE: Oh yeah.

LAURENT: Close to a volcano.

8.

BEATE: Phöbe had dragged me along.
             Because she needed me. Not to be nice.
             I'm not the girlfriend type.
             I didn't feel like being there.
             Garden parties are not my thing.
             But then. Then I was going to make the most of it.
             Eat a few ribs count a few clouds.
             With dancing flip-flops in front of me.
             I still remember. I was smiling because I was in love
             with a folding
             chair that was there.
             When Laurent came bursting into my life.
             Backwards from the dark of the hedge.
             I dropped a rib on the lawn.

LAURENT: Then she called me an idiot.

BEATE: I didn't want company.
             Him included.
             Watch where you're going you idiot.

9.

LAURENT: The casserole is done.
             She burns herself eating the letters.
             B and L.

BEATE: My finger tastes bitter. And sweet.
My tongue is pasty.
Cinnamon and sugar.
Is this cake or something.

LAURENT: B'stila.

BEATE: What.

LAURENT: Pie.

BEATE: I'll get some cutlery.

LAURENT: We'll use these.

BEATE: He means our fingers.
The first piece crumbles in my hand.
A crackling like tiny necks breaking.

LAURENT: Filo pastry.

BEATE: One two three four layers of dough.
In between meat.
The meat is sour.
The dough melts away on your tongue tastelessly.
Almonds break in the meat.
My tongue traces my upper row of teeth.
It's an electric contact.
An unusual coating.
The pain robs my sight.

LAURENT: She eats with her eyes closed.

BEATE: A ginger fibre is burning in my throat.
I drown it with wine from Fogo.
Our plates are now empty.
I didn't see him eat.

LAURENT: You're beautiful when you eat B'stila.

BEATE: Amazing. Your pie.

LAURENT: It's pigeon pie.

BEATE: Pigeons.

LAURENT: I fell in love with you from the very first moment.

10.

BEATE: I'm not that kind of girl.
          Everything about me droops a bit.
          My hair my eyes my upper lip.
          My overbite is not the cute and sensual kind.
          It's more like the other kind. The retarded kind.
          I like smoking pot eating and music.
          And could more or less skip the rest.
          I'm not that girl you fall in love with from the first
          moment.
          The first moment.
          Folding chair. Dusk.
          One of my pant legs was rolled up the other one
          wasn't.
          A blob of ketchup on my big toe.
          Laurent fell out of the hedge.
          Where did you come from.

LAURENT: Fogo.

BEATE: What.

LAURENT: Cape Verde. West Africa.

BEATE: I'd meant the hedge. But then. Then I noticed his that
          his hair was dyed and frizzy. His skin was dark almost
          black. And glistened like crazy in the glow of a string
          of lights.

11.

LAURENT: What are you doing.

BEATE: I'm puking pigeons asshole.

LAURENT: I don't see them flapping.

BEATE: I want to leave. Leave the bathroom the apartment.
          Leave this place and him. Then I remember that we're
          at my place.

LAURENT: I didn't know. That you're afraid of pigeons.

BEATE: I'm not afraid of pigeons.

LAURENT: If they're in casseroles you are.

BEATE: I'm not afraid.

LAURENT: Then on to the main course.

BEATE: Yeah. Let's fry up some spiders.

LAURENT: Yeah.

12.

BEATE: I didn't wish for anyone. To fall down at my feet in a garden. But now. Now that he was here. I offered him a toke.

LAURENT: No. No thanks. It makes me paranoid.

BEATE: He sat down in the grass next to me. Without being invited. I wanted to say. Leave me alone. And then I saw an ant crawl across his lower arm. And found it so beautiful. The path it took. What were you doing in the hedge.

LAURENT: Nature was calling. But then.

BEATE: Then what.

LAURENT: There was something there.

BEATE: What.

LAURENT: A spider.

BEATE: I looked over to the hedge. As if I could meet eyes with the spider.

LAURENT: A spider crawled over my dick.

BEATE: Oh so he's that kind of guy.
From West Africa.
Perfumed and wearing brand name T-shirts.
Diesel. G-Star. Adidas.
Calvin Klein jeans.
Who dyes his hair yellow and is afraid of spiders.

LAURENT: I've been here a long time. Since I was nine.

BEATE: He looked down at my big toe.
The one with the blob of ketchup and that's when it happened.
Maybe it had to do with the light or the grass.
Maybe it was all imagination all in my head all hallucination.

I know that happens sometimes.
But out of the blue sky the most beautiful prince of the party was
kneeling in front of me.
King of the garden.
Fallen at my feet.
Shiny skin.
Eyes black almonds.
Eyebrows short and thin.
Above them. Two creases. Vertical.
That stretched when he talked.
He spoke through heart lips. The colour of salmon.
White teeth pink tongue.
A scar on his left ear.
A sickle. White as snow in his dark skin.
I took a close look at him.
A very close look.
It was a face I wanted a magnifying glass for.
He was wearing a necklace.
The pendant hidden in his Diesel T-shirt.

13.

LAURENT: Uncle Armand taught me how to cook.

BEATE: Armand.

LAURENT: Armand took me to Germany.

BEATE: When you were nine.

LAURENT: Four chilli peppers. Two spring onions. Two sweet potatoes. Four okra. Two red peppers. One manioc bulb. One jar of peanut butter. Tomato paste. Want to see a photo. Of Armand.

BEATE: Your uncle.

LAURENT: My father.

BEATE: Your father's name is Armand too.

LAURENT: Pretty much everybody is Armand on Fogo.

BEATE: He pulls at the leather necklace. After seven weeks he's finally opening the pendant. Underneath the metal are two faces dark and worn. Who's the other person.

LAURENT: Cesária.

BEATE: Cesária.

LAURENT: My mother.

BEATE: She looks like a man your mother.

LAURENT: That's from the air. The lava dust. It weathers the skin.

BEATE: He chops onions cuts up the chilli peppers. Peels the sweet potato first then the manioc. He doesn't say a word. A vein is pulsing beneath his scar. Slicing through the green okra with the bread knife he cuts his thumb.

LAURENT: I almost forgot about the lamb.

BEATE: His thumb in my mouth. I taste onion and iron. With my tongue I pull a piece of chilli from the wound.

LAURENT: She looks at me. I look at her. Through kitchen-tears. The meat is in the duffel bag.

14.

BEATE: When it got dark in the garden I asked him about the scar.

LAURENT: A household injury.

BEATE: I noticed how the scar was losing its glow.

LAURENT: A clothes iron.

BEATE: I had imagined other things. Wilder things.

Machetes cannibals the claws of a predatory animal.

LAURENT: I'm Laurent.

BEATE: Laurent.
I'd never said the name Laurent before.
I'm Beate.

LAURENT: Beate.

BEATE: That's right. Beate. That's as much as you'll hear.

LAURENT: Are you always like this at parties.

BEATE: Like what.

LAURENT: So quiet keeping to yourself.

BEATE: The party is happening inside me. How about you.

LAURENT: I'm here because of Fred.

BEATE: Fred.

LAURENT: The DJ.

BEATE: The blind bat.

LAURENT: Fred is DJing tomorrow at the Bergdorf.

BEATE: The Bergdorf.

LAURENT: It's a club.

BEATE: Great.

LAURENT: Are you coming.

BEATE: No.

LAURENT: You definitely have to come.

BEATE: I'm not the club type.

LAURENT: If you don't come I'll die.

BEATE: You'll die no matter what.

LAURENT: Oh come on.

BEATE: No.

LAURENT: I'm on the guest list. Laurent and one guest.

BEATE: Aha. So it's like that is it. Come on No Please. In
             the end you say maybe and already you're lying. It's
             exactly discussions like these. That I try to avoid. But
             it wasn't like that. It didn't end up like that. I heard a
             See ya coming out of his salmon mouth. And suddenly
             I could imagine everything. Even that he might die.
             Tomorrow. Just because I didn't go to the Bergdorf.

15.

LAURENT: Here. Raw meat. Put your hand in it.

BEATE: No. Why.

LAURENT: Because it's like touching your internal organs. Your heart your kidneys your intestines.

BEATE: You're disgusting.

LAURENT: You're wonderful.

BEATE: He dumps it into the frying pan. The bits of lamb. I say his name. Laurent. Twice tenderly. But it's drowned out by the hissing of the oil. Everything disappears into a second pot. Chopped small. Green and red and yellow. He squeezes the tomato paste from the tube. Heaps peanut butter into the pot. Salt straight out of the box. Water from the tap. In a third pot rice is boiling.

LAURENT: So. Do you like okra.

BEATE: No idea.

LAURENT: Have a taste.

BEATE: The first kiss. Was unbelievable.

LAURENT: I haven't seen my parents in eight years.

BEATE: So. Do you miss them.

LAURENT: Try this.

BEATE: Green peel between his teeth. My tongue in the corner of his pink mouth.

LAURENT: Unbelievable.

16.

BEATE: At the Bergdorf.
Lost a bag of grass to the bouncer.
Elbowed teenagers out of my way.
Steam in my eyes. Neon light.
I didn't remember any of it.
The folding-chair-feeling.
That it cold be fatal and unbelievably sad to not go to the Bergdorf.
I saw Fred. The blind DJ.
His head tilted.
As if to see light of day in the club air.
No idea what I came here for.

I thought of the name I'd heard the day before.
Laurent.
I considered going home.
Watching TV eating a few peanuts maybe soaking my
feet.
That would be an evening well spent.
Then a hand touched my elbow.
I wait a second.
Blacking out.
White smoke in my mouth and nose.
A laser hits the palm of my hand.
A moment of absolute silence.
Absolute nothingness.
Slowly I turn.

17.

LAURENT: Beneath a sweet-potato-manioc-bulb-mountain.
Light-red sauce dark-brown meat.
Bell peppers and the okra peek out like bits of green
and red
salamander.
She has three spoonfuls.
After the third she peels off skin from the roof of her
mouth with her
tongue.

BEATE: My mouth is bleeding.

LAURENT: Eat some rice. It will cool it.

BEATE: I'm bleeding you asshole.

LAURENT: How about you. Would you miss me.

18.

BEATE: His dark dark face.
The bright sickle on his ear.
Lips pink.
His hair a yellow helmet in the black light.
His jeans are tight. Combat boots on his feet.
His T-shirt white like a fluffy cloud over the Ivory

Coast.
Kind of ridiculous. Your outfit.

LAURENT: Glad you could make it.

BEATE: My smile takes two minutes to appear. Then. There it is.
Absolutely content. Stretching across my face.
On my lips in my eyes in my blood.
The music has gotten louder. Harder.
He says something.
What.
Talk louder.

LAURENT: Raw Garage.

BEATE: Then we kissed.
And I knew. There would never be words.
That could describe my happiness and my fear.
I knew any attempt at them would be a joke.
Anyone would laugh. Me included.
I would have said we were underwater.
My lips wrapped in silk.
His fingers travelling over my neck.
Like a boat travelling through soft water.
Right from the start I was afraid of losing him.

19.

LAURENT: When she stands up in the warm kitchen she can't feel her legs anymore.

BEATE: Poison.
Wouldn't be the first time.
That kind of thing happens.
You never know.
We still don't know each other that well.

LAURENT: She feels the warmth.
At first in her forehead then in her neck.
It flows through her spine and back into her legs.

BEATE: Your island grub tore the fuck out of my mouth.

LAURENT: I carried her.
Through the kitchen to her room to her bed.
She's doing fine.

Her mouth is warm not torn apart.
Peanuts are sleeping in her throat.
Wine on her breath.
My hand sticks to her forehead.

BEATE: Don't get carried away.

LAURENT: Uncle Armand brought me all of this. The wine and
            the okra.

BEATE: Are you trying to poison me or something.

LAURENT: He went to visit my parents on Fogo.

BEATE: I'm hot.

LAURENT: My parents are hairdressers.

BEATE: Can't you see how hot I am.

LAURENT: They have their own salon.
            A set of chairs at the foot of the volcano.
            La Coiffure d'Eternité.

BEATE: Laurent.

LAURENT: The Hairdo of Eternity.

BEATE: Kiss me.

LAURENT: They're 63. Both of them.
            They have magic hands. The paws of barbers.
            They cut, braid, twirl, roll, smoothen, tease.
            Shave stars into necks. Implant magma into scalps.
            They've never gone to school for it. They were born
            with it.
            They're magicians. Hair poets. The only hairdressers
            on the island.

20.

BEATE: The reason I didn't stop smoking weed.
            I don't think I could have coped. Being sober.
            Sober everything would have been too big for me.
            The love the happiness. What was foreign about him.
            I had a million questions.
            What was it like on your island. Do they all look like
            you.
            Who are your parents.

Did you sleep in a wooden hut.
Do you have antelopes on your island. Malaria. Rainy
seasons.
Aren't you homesick.
I didn't ask any of this.
I was sitting next to him in the subway when two guys
tossed a
banana in his lap.
He didn't say a word.
He talked about parties about school.
About guest lists. A jacket he was going to buy.
We were together seven weeks.
He never talked about Fogo.
I found a stack of papers in his apartment.
Next to the telephone.
Donation forms. Leaflets. Fact sheets. Petitions.
What's this.

LAURENT: West Africa stuff.

BEATE: What are you going to do with it.

LAURENT: It's not mine. It's Albert's.

BEATE: Who's Albert.

LAURENT: Dork from school.
Mr. Extracurricular. Started the West Africa Outreach
Group.

BEATE: Well that's pretty interesting right.

LAURENT: I can give you Albert's number if you want.

BEATE: Do you want me to sign somewhere.

LAURENT: I want to sleep with you.

BEATE: But I don't want to. Not yet.

LAURENT: Why not.

BEATE: We've still got time.
That's what I said.
A week before he cooked for me.
We've still got time.

21.

LAURENT: My Uncle came back from Fogo last week.

BEATE: Does that matter now.

LAURENT: My parents aren't doing well.

BEATE: Don't they have any doctors on your island.

LAURENT: It's one big volcano.

BEATE: I want to kiss you.

LAURENT: My parents live too close to it.
           They breathe soil and drink smoke.
           My father's got a bag of lava instead of a lung.
           His breathing is louder than a dryer hood.
           My mother chugs wine and sings.
           And spits black stones into her customers' hair.
           My uncle was there.

           He says the salon is going to pieces. The whole island
           is going to
           pieces.
           People have lice in their hair.
           Are covered in scars form razors.
           Nothing shines anymore. Nothing.

BEATE: Quit that Fogo bullshit will you.

LAURENT: They need a hairdresser there.

BEATE: Stop it.

LAURENT: They need me.

BEATE: You.

LAURENT: I've got to go.

BEATE: To Fogo.

LAURENT: Yes.

BEATE: Man fuck off that's bullshit.

LAURENT: I have to take over the salon.

BEATE: You're not a hairdresser. Just look at you.

LAURENT: I inherited it. I've got it in my hands.
            I'm going to get the colour taken out of my hair.

BEATE: Stop.

LAURENT: They're my parents.

BEATE: You don't even know them.

LAURENT: They need me there.

BEATE: I need you here.

LAURENT: Where are you going.

BEATE: To get the pudding.

LAURENT: Come here.

BEATE: Why.

LAURENT: I want to sleep with you.

BEATE: Get the fuck out.

LAURENT: She goes to the kitchen.
            Her knees are soft her legs heavy. She opens the fridge
            and burps.
            A piece of okra in her mouth.
            Salt and peel.
            She swallows it a second time.
            When she comes back to the room. Gripping the
            pudding firmly in her
            hand.
            I'm gone.

BEATE: That's it. That's the whole story.
            Laurent cooked for me.
            Made me puke cry fall.
            Told me about Africa. About hairdressers and
            volcanoes.
            And then he got the fuck out.
            I poured the pudding into a bowl and ate it.
            Found five prunes in the yellow mass.
            I thought of cockroaches and didn't chew.
            Tears only came with the last of the five. Which got
            stuck in my
            throat.
            A cork a seal a cockroach-ending.
            I never saw him again.

	Someone I know ran into his uncle. Who said. Laurent is a
	hairdresser on Fogo now.
	Somebody else said Uncle Armand doesn't even exist.

ALBERT: saw Laurent in a steakhouse downtown.

ALBERT: thinks. Laurent is a grill master now.
I don't know I don't care.
All I know is that he's gone. At the foot of one fucking volcano or the other.
All I have left of him I carry around with me.
In my mouth.
The peanut butter the lemon kisses.
The salt and the slime.
Cinnamon and pigeon shit.
He said. I want to sleep with you.
I told him. To get the fuck out.
So.
Would you have stayed. If we'd done it.

LAURENT: No.

BEATE: Why should I have done it then.

LAURENT: For love for Christ's sake. For love.

NIGHTBLIND

by Darja Stocker
Translated by Philip Thorne

Further Copyright Information

Nightblind

Characters

LEYLA

MO

MOTHER

RICO

PLACES:

ABOVE THE TRACKS

LEYLA'S HOME

NIGHTBLIND WAS FIRST PERFORMED IN THE UK IN NOVEMBER 2008, AT THEATRE CAFE, UNICORN THEATRE, LONDON.

This play came about through the support of the new writing program 'Dramenprozessor' at Theater in der Winkelwiese in Zurich (direction: Stephan Roppel and Erika Altorfer).

Note on the play's dramaturgy

Nightblind makes use of an intricate dramaturgy in which past and present seem to intermingle. It presents great opportunities for directors to explore the different levels of address at play.

It is not so much a straight forward flashback, as a play that takes place in the memories of Mo and Leyla. The play is their attempt at working through a story that has only just happened to them, but whose huge implications they have not yet realised. And so in order to reflect on and position themselves towards what they have experienced, they have to tell their story to the audience.

The first scene shows Mo and Leyla addressing both each other and the audience. It's as though they need the audience as a partner in figuring out the string of events that has brought them here. As Mo and Leyla find a way into the telling of their story, a silent shift takes place by the end of which they are inhabiting the story rather than narrating it.

By the end of the play Mo and Leyla have come full circle. They have revisited all the stages of their journey, and only now are they aware of how far they have come, how much has changed. Leyla has freed herself from her emotional dependency to BULL. A new relationship has begun with Mo, one based not on servility but freedom. The play has brought Mo and Leyla up to the present and now it is up to the audience to imagine their future...

Philip Thorne

34 OR 0

*Mo and Leyla lie outside the shed. They are bruised
from the fight.*

1 SPARKS

In front of the shed.

LEYLA: At the beginning sparks flew.

MO: Sparks?

LEYLA: Yeah. Sparks.

MO: You mean fists. Fists flew.

LEYLA: It was at that party. I'm a match, he's a matchbox.

MO: I'm a flint, she's a flint.
We had to bang our heads together so something could happen.

LEYLA: Fire and sparks.

MO: I just wouldn't put it like that.

LEYLA: No?

MO: No. But something *did* flare up between us.

LEYLA: I asked him what his name was.

MO: Mo.

LEYLA: Mo? What kind of a name's that?

MO: A made up name.

LEYLA: You can't do that!

MO: Why not.

LEYLA: Were they trying to big you up?

MO: Who?

LEYLA: Your mum and dad, duh.
They wanted to make you stand out.

MO: P 'raps they should have tried 'Napoleon' then.

LEYLA: MO.
Sounds like a weirdo.
MO.
Good to shout though:
MOOOOOOOOOOOO/ OOOOOOOOOO

MO: Stop it!

LEYLA: MOOOOOOOOOOOO –

MO: Stop it!

LEYLA: I know why your mum and dad gave you this name.
So whoever meets you goes:
What kind of name's that?
Where does it come from?
What does it mean?
They want to force everybody into telling you how special, interesting
and exciting you are.
I bet that every day you have to live up to this amazing
Mo.
Don't you see, your mum and dad are manipulating your identity!

MO: Well what's your name
I asked.

LEYLA: Leyla.

MO: Leyla means night.

LEYLA: How d'you know?

MO: You're not the only one with that name.

LEYLA: I only know one other.

MO: Leila Khaled.

LEYLA: You know her?

MO: Everyone knows a terrorist.

LEYLA: She's not a terrorist. She's a freedom fighter.

MO: She hijacked a plane and threw a hand-grenade at the passengers –

LEYLA: Which didn't go off!

178

MO: She's a trained suicide bomber –

LEYLA: She's been building fresh water pipelines for thirty years, she's saved the lives of thousands of women and children –

I wanted to punch him in the –

MO: The first spark had flown.

LEYLA: Just so you know, I was named after her.

MO: So your parents had a special plan for you too then?

LEYLA: What do you want here anyway?
I asked.

MO: My brother's a bouncer here.

LEYLA: So you follow him around to all the parties?

MO: Yes – No.
It's the first time today.

LEYLA: I can tell.

(Silence.)

I asked him what he did.

MO: Nothing.

LEYLA: What d'you mean 'nothing'.

MO: Nothing.

LEYLA: You have to get up to something?

MO: I stay home.

LEYLA: And at home?
What do you do at home?

*(**MO** is silent.)*

Eat
Play games
Lift weights
Watch TV, DVD, MTV
Wank
Sleep
Chat

Surf
Drink
Smoke
Get high –

MO: I distil.

LEYLA: Sorry?

MO: I distil.
            I said.

LEYLA: What's that? Distilling?

2 YOU'VE PULLED

MO: She pulled –

LEYLA: Shit no –

MO: Yes you did. You pulled, took me to your shed –

LEYLA: *You* took my hand.

MO: She took my hand.

LEYLA: *You* took my hand.

MO: *You* took/ my hand.

LEYLA: *He* took my hand –

MO: No, you –

LEYLA: He took my hand.

MO: No/ you

LEYLA: you/

MO AND LEYLA: took my hand.

   (Pause)

LEYLA: He took my hand because he sees nothing in the dark.

MO: I don't see *nothing*.

3 HAND

By the tracks.

LEYLA: It's sweaty.

MO: Don't worry.

LEYLA: It's always like that.

MO: Don't worry.

LEYLA: Disgusting.

MO: Don't worry.

LEYLA: You think it's disgusting.

MO: No. I don't.

(MO clutches her hand tighter. LEYLA starts.)

Sorry!

LEYLA: Don't worry.

MO: Did I –

LEYLA: No.

MO: I'm –

LEYLA: Don't worry.

4 ABOVE THE TRACKS

The high voltage wires suspended in the red morning glow.

LEYLA: We've arrived.

(Pause.)

Nice isn't it?

(Silence.)

MO: Do you often come here?

LEYLA: After I've been spraying.

MO: What do you spray?

LEYLA: Over there, in green, I did that.

(MO searches.)

Green and yellow, over there.

*(**MO** searches.)*

Over there, top floor.

MO: This –

LEYLA: No, over there, in yellow and green.
Yellow and green!

MO: I can't see yellow or green.

LEYLA: Are you blind?

MO: Yes. Colour-blind.

LEYLA: Over there –

MO: Don't you believe me?

LEYLA: Huh?

MO: I'm colour-blind.

LEYLA: You're kidding right?

MO: I inherited it from my dad.
Like a TV set fifty years ago.

LEYLA: The thing in black and white then.
Next to the smoking chimney. The highest.

MO: Massive.

LEYLA: I Painted it with my mate.
He took me on his shoulders for the most difficult bits.

MO: Were you scared?

LEYLA: No.
Of course I was scared.
See the writing on the chimney, way up there?

MO: Castle in the C...

LEYLA: We couldn't finish it.
Now everyone who sees it has to imagine the last five letters:
L-O-U-D-S
Clouds.
Nobody is allowed to paint over that.

(Silence.)

MO: Has he been here?

LEYLA: Who?

MO: Your mate.

LEYLA: No, never.

5 BULL

LEYLA's room.

LEYLA: BULL – I don't know where he is
         It was eight nights ago
         in his flat
         where he –
         Since then he's not called
         I'm
         lying
         with open eyes
         waiting
         waiting
         for him to give me a sign
         an answer
         a message anything
         Like he usually does
         But this time
         I hear nothing

         This time it's –
         As though he's fallen
         headfirst
         killed
         whilst spraying

6 BUSTA RHYMES

Table. LEYLA, MOTHER, RICO.

MOTHER: Go on.
         Ask her.

RICO: You coming to the Busta Rhymes concert with me?

LEYLA: When is it?

MOTHER: Saturday evening.

LEYLA: I can't.

RICO: See, see, mum.

MOTHER: Can't you put it off,
         whatever it is?

LEYLA: Nope.

MOTHER: This once?

LEYLA: Nope.

   (Pause.)

MOTHER: The one time he goes to the trouble of asking you.

   *(**LEYLA** is silent)*

   Where do you need to go so desperately?

   *(**LEYLA** is silent)*

RICO: But we already have the tickets –

MOTHER: Forget it. She thinks it's too UNCOOL to do anything with
         her brother.
         Embarrassing, your brother, isn't he?
         Not to mention your mother.
         We should be grateful she's still sitting down to eat with us.

RICO: She hates me.

LEYLA: *(Mimicking RICO.)* She hates me, she hates me, my sister
         hates me –

MOTHER: Stop that. You know what he means.

LEYLA: Why's he asking me anyway? No other loser would go out
         with –

MOTHER: Because it would make him happy. If you could be more
         –

LEYLA: Why don't you go. Or dad.
         A proper 'father and son' evening.

MOTHER: Daddy can't.

7 LEYLA

MO: Leyla
I like sitting up here with her
Because
When she looks at me
my head spins
and I smile
can't stop smiling
and she –
Suddenly the corners of her mouth twitch
she's overcome
I wonder if she goes red
I've heard that if a woman laughs and goes red
she wants you

When I want to put my hand on her skin
she pulls away from it

8 LEFTOVERS

RICO's plate is empty. LEYLA's plate is full. MOTHER has finished.

MOTHER: *(To RICO)* Before you help yourself ask if anyone else
wants any more.

RICO: Fat chance. *(Pointing at LEYLA's plate)* She hasn't even
touched it.

MOTHER: Don't you like it?

RICO: She wants to get skinny. For her boyfriend –

LEYLA: Shut up!

RICO: See?
She's a bitch.
Hormones gone crazy.
That's what you said, isn't it mum?

MOTHER: Me?

RICO: Crazy hormones.

MOTHER: I –

RICO: You did! You said –

MOTHER: I didn't/ say

LEYLA: I'm finished. Can I get up? *(She gets up).*

RICO: No. Wait till we're finished. And eat up. What a waste!

MOTHER: *(To LEYLA)* Don't you want to eat *anything*?

RICO: She's been on a diet ever since she's been fucking this Mo.

MOTHER: Rico, that's enough.

RICO: What?
             What did I do?
             What the fuck did I do?

             (LEYLA walks towards the door.)

             It's your fat arse you're worried about isn't it Leyla?

             (LEYLA doesn't reply.)

MOTHER: *(To LEYLA.)* Come on! Defend Yourself! You've usually got the gift of the gab!

RICO: Sorry sis, I love you sis, sorry, sorry, sorry!

9 PADLOCK

Above the tracks.

MO: Been spraying?

LEYLA: I don't spray anymore.

MO: Why not?

             (LEYLA is silent.)

             What about your mate? Does he still spray?

LEYLA: I couldn't give a shit about him.

MO: You're mad at him?

             (Silence.)

LEYLA: Why would you care?

(Silence.)

What about you. Been 'distilling'?

MO: I've turned my room into a secret laboratory and secured it with a padlock.

LEYLA: A padlock?

MO: Yep. It's got three different number codes and an automatic catch.
When I've finished work at the garage
I go straight up to my room
and lock up.
It's really cosy since I've got the padlock.
When I need a piss,
I stand on the windowsill,
so I don't have to go out.

LEYLA: You're totally mental.

MO: The granny next door called the police.
A moment later
three fire engines with screaming sirens pull up.
The firemen stretch out a rescue net.
'I'm gonna piss!' I yell down at them.
But they're far too busy fumbling with the net to listen.
'I'm just pissing' I yelled again,
as loud as I could.
Again and again. Getting angrier and angrier.
I couldn't stop pissing with all the excitement.
I tried. I concentrated.
But the piss kept coming.
They put a ladder to my window.
What the fuck's going on I thought.
Then a bloody psychiatrist comes clambering up.
Gets a real close up.
Asks me why I'm yelling 'I'm going to jump.'

He advised me to shut up and get off the windowsill.
Wanted to be done with it as quickly as possible.

(Pause.)

LEYLA: A granny like that'd really get on my tits.
Snooping into other people's business, just 'cos she's past it.
I'm glad we don't have any neighbours.

MO: What, so nobody cares if you jump from a window?

LEYLA: You weren't going to jump from the –

MO: She didn't have her glasses on.

LEYLA: She just thought it was a bit weird of you
balancing around up there with your trousers open.
So she called the police and told them there was someone about to commit suicide.

MO: Na. I think she just wanted to see me pissing on the cops.

(Pause.)

LEYLA: Why?

MO: Her husband was a cop.
A detective.

LEYLA: How d'you know?

MO: I know her. Used to go to her place a lot.

There's a little wall you can walk on just under our window.
They were planning to build balconies there but never did.
When I was little I used to run along this wall,
round and round the courtyard,
and counted how many times I'd pass my window.
When I was worn out I'd sit,
dangle my feet
and watch the children play down below.

LEYLA: Why didn't you go down and join them?

MO: I preferred watching. Bit like the granny.

LEYLA: But you were a kid.

MO: Even so.
She's called Edith.

She used to make cake and left some for me on the wall
under her window.
She had a room full of books.
After school I'd climb through my window,
scramble along the wall straight to her place,
and sit on the floor next to her big rocking chair.
She read stories to me.
When she went to the loo, I carried on reading. Out loud.
I didn't know you could read silently.
One day she only pretended to go to the loo and listened
to me.
From that day on
I was allowed to take the books back home with me.
School didn't interest me. Instead of doing homework
I went to Edith's. With her I could talk about war
and what happens after you die,
justice and her husband's many cases
which he would never have solved without her help.
I had to be gone before he woke from his afternoon kip.
When I was ten
she lent me the camera he'd used as a detective.
She said if I figured out how it worked
I could keep it.
I didn't go to school for two days.
Then I'd cracked it.
I nicked some tin foil from the kitchen and blacked out
my windows with it.
I left a little hole in the centre where a ray of light could
shine through.
On the opposite wall of my room
a reflection of the courtyard appeared.
The trees, the slope, the swing, Edith's window.
Everything upside-down.
I waited for her to come out into the yard
and see my blacked out window.
I imagined how she'd wave at me
upside down
because she'd know
that inside I'd be sitting,

watching.

LEYLA: So, after this she let you keep the camera.

MO: She never came out.
Her husband did.
With a rifle from his cupboard.
Stormed outside holding it by the barrel as if it was a club.
I sat in the dark of my room
staring at Edith's window reflected on my wall
until the sun went down.
But there wasn't a flicker.
Soon after her husband died.

LEYLA: Perhaps she killed him?

(Pause.)

Why did she call the police?

MO: Dunno.
To take her mind off things.

10 SADOMASOCHISM

RICO: You into SM?

LEYLA: Shut up.

RICO: You're sick.

LEYLA: Me?

RICO: Mum said.

LEYLA: Whatever.

RICO: 'Nobody can so much as touch you' she said.

LEYLA: Nobody has to touch me.

RICO: Act like you're mental.
She said.
Like she'd mistreated you.
She finds this attitude annoying.
This 'over the top, immature attitude.'
She said so to dad.

Said you're trying to big yourself up.

Said she can't wait for 'that phase to be over.'

LEYLA: Liar.

RICO: She's fed up. With you.

(LEYLA is silent.)

She can't help it since you've been like this.

LEYLA: Been like what?

(RICO is silent.)

Been like what?

RICO: Like... this.

LEYLA: What did she say about you huh?

RICO: She didn't say anything about me.

LEYLA: Nothing about what you're like?

RICO: No.

LEYLA: Didn't say you're a sad fucking chauvinist Arsehole –

RICO: No.

LEYLA: – who goes around with a knuckle-duster threatening little boys?

(RICO is silent.)

That's what they say about you.

RICO: So? She believes in me.

(Silence.)

LEYLA: Go on. If you're so eager. Tell her.

RICO: What?

LEYLA: About my back. Tell her.

RICO: Tell her yourself!

11 ROOM NEXT DOOR

LEYLA's room.

Gone without a trace
His flat is empty and nobody knows a thing

I had to
call his mother

She swallows when she hears my name
She knows where he is
But won't tell me
He needs his rest

Rest
Who from

She wants to hang up
isn't comfortable talking to me
But I
persist
it's urgent
I have something to tell him
It's important
Her voice
hardens
she's scared
of me
I remind her of the night he still lived with them
in the room next door
that night two years ago when it happened for the first
time
when I cried for help
so it echoed through the whole house
and she and her husband
in the room next door
pretended not to hear
because they were shit scared
of him

That was gutless
He inherited that from them

12 MONSTER

MOTHER: His name's Mo?

LEYLA: He's not my boyfriend.

MOTHER: I just hope he's better for you.

LEYLA: Better for me?

MOTHER: Better than that last one.

>   (*LEYLA* is silent.)

>   He did you no good.

LEYLA: You know what's good for me?

MOTHER: I'm your mother.

LEYLA: You don't know a thing!

MOTHER: Is that what you think.

LEYLA: What do *you* know about me and: *'that last one'*?
    See! You don't even know his name!

MOTHER: Because you hid him from me.
    As if I were a monster./ Or he was.

LEYLA: Because it's none of your business!

MOTHER: If you're in that kind of a mood Leyla,
    it is my business.
    If you take out your frustration about these guys on us
    It is my business.

LEYLA: It's not about guys!

MOTHER: Then tell me what it *is*!

>   (*LEYLA* is silent.)

>   Fine. You don't want to tell me. *(Turns to leave.)*

LEYLA: All you want is a sensation for dad, some gossip, a
    massive crisis, 'cos otherwise you've got nothing to say to
    each other.

MOTHER: No wonder you can't find anyone Leyla.
Nobody wants a face like that.

13 BRAINY

Above the tracks.

LEYLA: You're so brainy.

(Pause.)

They proud?

MO: Who?

LEYLA: Your mum and dad, of course.

MO: Yeah. I guess.

LEYLA: Mine would be. They'd tell everyone.
Set up a website:
www – dot – help – our – son – is – brainy – as – hell
– dot – com.

(Silence.)

Mum once wrote an article about brainy kids.
Said they need to go to special schools
which really challenge them.
Especially the girls, because they always pretend to be as dim
as the rest of the herd. It's a solidarity thing, she said.
Why don't you go to a special –

MO: 'Cos at my place being clever doesn't make you 'special'.

LEYLA: That's what your dad says?

MO: You wouldn't understand.

LEYLA: You think he wouldn't manage without you, right?

MO: I'm working on this sensor.
It'll help him at the garage. It works like a digital camera.
It measures the light intensity of every pixel and works out
the colour.

He just has to aim it at a car and he can read the name
on the screen.
That way he can give the customers information without
looking at the serial numbers. And read the traffic lights
on the street.
Maybe then he'll stop patrolling the garage at night.

14 A PRESENT

LEYLA's room. She's getting changed. Her body is bruised.

LEYLA: He's back
Suddenly he's standing at my door

He's been to a clinic
belongs to a friend of his dad's
won't say anymore

He just stands there
with his dumbo ears
and looks at me
tender
as though he'd always been proud of me

He's sorry
he says
he's sorry
about what happened
on that night

I want to spit in his face punch him leave him standing
there
with his stupid present in his rucksack

Run away now and for ever
But instead
I remain standing
nailed to the spot
staring

wondering
why it's happening all over
His arms
wrap around me
he pulls me to his chest
and once more it's like
I'm a baby bird
fallen from its nest and retrieved
warm and soft
his smell deep inside me

He's got something for me
not a stupid dress
A CD
Not any CD
One with a booklet
printed it himself
All our graffiti on glossy paper

We drive over to his flat
listen to it
A brilliant mix of all the songs
that make my heart race

How could he know this
I never listen with him
He made it for me
Not for the bitch I –
for the real me

I know the real him too
He's the most tender person I know

15 SOMETHING'S DIFFERENT

Above the tracks.

MO: You done something with your hair?

LEYLA: No.

MO: I'm sure you've –

LEYLA: No.

(*MO stares at her.*)

I've got to go.

MO: Now?

LEYLA: School.

MO: Tonight?

LEYLA: Can't.

MO: Busy?

LEYLA: Yes.

16 FUCKING CUNT

*The table is laid for four. **FATHER** is absent.*

RICO: I'm never going back to that shit-hole!

LEYLA: You can't go back. They've expelled you.

RICO: Leyla, please.

LEYLA: What? It's true!

RICO: Just 'cos of that teacher wanker.

LEYLA: (*To **MOTHER**.*) He's a friend of yours isn't he? From uni?

(*MOTHER is silent.*)

You could always try bribery. A thousand more each term –

RICO: Shut the fuck up.

LEYLA: – they might decide to put up with him then.

RICO: Shut up you cunt.

MOTHER: Rico.

RICO: (*To Leyla.*)
        Cunt
        Cunt
        Cunt

Cunt
Cunt
Fucking Filthy Cunt!

MOTHER: That's enough!

(*RICO* kicks *MOTHER* in the legs and leaves.)

(Calls after him.) Rico! (Gives up.)

(Silence.)

LEYLA: Has this happened before?

(*MOTHER* doesn't reply.)

Didn't you write something about this once,
about violence and women and how there are still some women
who endure it out of sheer kindness,
you did mum, didn't you?

MOTHER: Do you have any idea what *real* violence is Leyla?

(Silence.)

LEYLA: Where's dad.

MOTHER: Nightshift.

LEYLA: Since when does he do nightshifts?

MOTHER: There was an emergency.

LEYLA: Since when does he do nightshifts?

17 CRY

LEYLA's room.

LEYLA: When he comes close to me
I shut off
I don't do it on purpose
I really don't do it on purpose
I hold my breath
bite my lips
so he won't notice
how tense I am

Then
he's sitting
depressed
with twitching eyelids
his mouth
crude
and small
being with him makes me want to cry
makes me want to cry

I feel it again
The cloggy broth inside my stomach
how it lies there
cold heavy and stinking
splashing up to my chest
stowing up
pressing
my throat
far too tight
retching
no use
it becomes silent
as though I've been swallowed up
to be somewhere different

I wake with a jolt
suddenly noticing
how I'm lying there
paralysed
with a hollow stare
and a stupid grin in place of my face
I wish
it would explode
the toxic broth inside me
tear me to shreds
eat out my innards
until I no longer feel anything

His warmth
I can no longer stand it
I roll over to the edge
far out to the edge
and think of Mo
whether he's awake
now

18 DEPENDANT

Above the tracks.

LEYLA: He's been my only one.

MO: Was it serious?

LEYLA: Three years.

MO: Where did the two of you meet –

LEYLA: Same club the two of us –

MO: I see.

LEYLA: He used to DJ there.

(Pause.)

You know that big building behind the park?

MO: Yeah, the monastery.

LEYLA: It's not a monastery.

MO: What is it?

LEYLA: It's a private clinic. Looney bin for the rich.
Belongs to his mum and dad.

(Pause.)

They thought I was a 'bad influence' on him.

(MO is silent.)

I made him dependant.
When I'm not with him,
even when I just go to get a drink,
he gets such pain that –
I haven't met anyone else since I've been with –

MO: But you're no longer with –

LEYLA: No.

MO: How long?

LEYLA: A while.

MO: Who broke –

LEYLA: I did.

19 DISGUST

MOTHER is standing at the mirror making herself up. LEYLA observes her.

MOTHER: What are you staring at me like this for?

LEYLA: You really don't see that you disgust him even more like this do you?

MOTHER: What on earth do you mean?

LEYLA: He has to pull himself together when you touch him.

MOTHER: Leyla, what are you talking about?

LEYLA: When you put your arms around him
            he goes all tense,
            and whenever you try to kiss him
            he turns away.
            Even your voice disgusts him.
            Whenever you're talking,
            he shuts off completely
            just stares at his plate.

MOTHER: Your father is dog-tired when he comes home in the evenings.

LEYLA: You disgust him mum.

            (MOTHER says nothing.)

            You never used to tart yourself up for him.
            Not like like this.
            Did you mum?

MOTHER: What –

LEYLA: It's embarrassing.

> Putting on a show like this.
> It doesn't make it better.
> It makes it worse.
> It's disgusting.

MOTHER: The way you chase after the guys Leyla.
Like a desperate little bitch.

LEYLA: I know mum.

20 PRINCESS

LEYLA's room. LEYLA bangs the back of her head against the wall.

LEYLA: Every morning afternoon evening
and in between
he calls
princess
my darling
princess
Tell me how strong your love is
Like yesterday
two days ago
a week ago
a month ago

Confess
Have you met somebody else
Please don't
go away tonight
You'll make me sick
The pain is unbearable
when you go
Don't you dare
go away tonight
Princess
You'll break my –

Three years every morning afternoon evening
and in between

being with you makes me want to cry
makes me want to cry

I love you
Nobody will ever love you like me
nobody and nowhere in the world
I'm sorry about –
I'm sorry
It only happened
because of how much I
because you
You torture me
I'm in unbearable pain
because of you
I'm sorry about –
Never again
That's a promise
Never
I'm sorry

A CD
a CD
not any CD
one with a booklet
printed it himself
all our graffiti on glossy paper
Fucking shit
for me
he made it for me
for the real me
I know the real him too
I know

21 HAPPY

Above the tracks.

MO: Have you been crying?

You've been crying.

LEYLA: *(Angry.)* Why? Are my eyes red?

MO: I can't see red eyes.

LEYLA: 'Cos I don't have any.

MO: Even if you did –

LEYLA: Yes, I know.

MO: So. Why did you cry?

LEYLA: I didn't cry!

MO: You did.

LEYLA: I didn't.

MO: So you're happy.

LEYLA: Yep.

MO: You're totally happy.

LEYLA: Yep.

> *(Pause.)*

MO: Leyla, stop this,
         I know you're –

LEYLA: All you know
         is that my name is Leyla
         and I sprayed that crap over there.
         You know nothing.

MO: About what?

22 SOMEBODY ELSE

LEYLA: I saw dad.
         At the station.

         He's with somebody else.

         Black hair.
         Boots and a mini skirt.

He kissed her.

I almost puked.

(Silence.)

MOTHER: I thought he'd told you.

(Silence.)

You know things haven't been –

LEYLA: So what.

(Silence.)

MOTHER: We decided not to say anything to Rico.
About this woman.

LEYLA: Why?

MOTHER: We're concerned about him.
Daddy and I.

LEYLA: I'm
'concerned'
about you mum.
D'you think, I don't notice.
D'you think, I don't see them.
The things you take, so you don't get hungry.
So you can sleep.
So you don't feel like sex.
So you're cheerful.

I think, you've finally lost it, mum.
I've had it up to here.
Your dogged persistence in everything you do.
Sport.
Work.
Cooking.
The way you try it on with dad.

Didn't expect this of you mum.
You said never to conform.

That's what you fought for,
isn't it,
that's what you took to the streets for,
isn't it mum?

MOTHER: I never said don't conform, I said you should keep your
identity –

I'm not talking to you about it.

LEYLA: You don't talk to anyone about it.

MOTHER: You wouldn't/ understand it. You're too –

LEYLA: 'Understand it'/ 'immature', I know.

MOTHER: Not just that.

LEYLA: You can tell dad, I don't want to see him again.
Doesn't have to come home, not for me.
Tell him that.

I don't want to see him again, you hear me?

MOTHER: Yes. Leyla.

23 LOVE

Above the tracks.

(Silence.)

LEYLA: Every day
you lie under these cars at the garage.
You lie under these cars
and dream of becoming a physicist.
That's what you dream about,
don't you?

  (MO doesn't reply.)

I bet that's what you're dreaming of
every minute of every hour of every day.
And your work just feels like total shit,
but you carry on and on and on,
trying not to let anything on
because you're scared
that your dad won't want you any more
when he notices
that you're different from how he –

MO: I'm not different.

LEYLA: You want to be a physicist. Go tell him.

MO: You don't know what he's like.

LEYLA: I can imagine.

MO: No.

LEYLA: You'll never forgive yourself for not having the guts –
You can't look yourself in the eye,
I know this feeling Mo.
You're ashamed.
Deeply ashamed.
It'll kill you,
you've got to have the balls
to act!

MO: You're talking about me?

LEYLA: You'll see.

> If you don't have the guts
> to break out of this,
> little clumps of self-loathing will grow inside you,
> like tumours,
> they'll destroy everything,
> you'll have to thrash them out of your system,
> so when someone comes and asks who you are,
> Your spine doesn't just crumple up.

MO: Thanks. I'm not going to 'crumple up.'

LEYLA: Go home and tell him.

MO: I can't.

LEYLA: Why not?

MO: We have an agreement.

LEYLA: What kind of agreement?

(MO doesn't reply.)

> I know that kind of crap.
> Don't fall for it.

MO: You really think you know?

LEYLA: Do it. Tell him what you really want.

MO: No.

LEYLA: You're a wimp!
> You're a fucking wimp.
> I don't get you.

MO: Yeah, that's right Leyla,
> go on,
> play the rebel!
> Cool, huh, playing a bit of ghetto?
> Like in a movie: 'from the very bottom to the very top.'
> Lucky,
> that if you ever *really* slipped up,
> you'd just have to give a little wave,
> and right on cue,
> your great parents,
> your great 'we're fighting for a better world' parents
> would rush in to rescue you –

LEYLA: My parents won't –

MO: Oh come on Leyla.
           There's a place for you at private school till you're thirty,
           just in case you really screw up. Because your mummy
           and daddy
           don't believe you can be anything without a degree,
           they're just too fucking hypocritical to admit it:
            'My daughter, she's allowed to be anything,
           she can be a lesbian, a bricklayer, marry a Muslim.'
           But then (oh what a surprise)
           she becomes a journalist just like her mother.
           Or a doctor. At least mine are honest.
           At least they have that.

24 ALL MADE UP

MO: I see her standing at this bar
           this bar in this fucking club
           this club which I'd never go to
           and I know straight away
           that something's not right
           Her hair
           fresh
           styled
           curled
           so bloody fake
           When she laughs she scares me
           She doesn't recognise me
           with these eyes
           drawn on
           And lips
           stuck on
           for him
           new trousers shoes little jacket
           for him
           he comes as I want to go to her
           he comes and pulls her toward him
           without looking at her

All for him
He grabs her by the scruff of the neck like a rabbit
presses her against the bar so her back bends over
and sticks his disgusting tongue in her mouth

25 NO LUNCH

*Afternoon. The table is laid out for four. The **FATHER** is absent.*
***LEYLA** is in her room.*

MOTHER: Leyla!

(Pause.)

LEYLA: It'll
        get
        cold!

(Long pause.)

        LUNCH!

(Pause.)

*(**MOTHER** grabs a rubbish bag. She throws one plate
after another into it. **RICO** hands over his plate too,
finally she throws away her own plate and even the
pan.)*

26 BLIND

LEYLA: It started off so well
       When I tell him I want to leave the club
       go out
       talk with him
       he agrees straight away

       We sat on his bed
       BULL and I
       he even looked me in the eyes
       when I said it

Silence
he'd seen it coming

I go to the door
he grabs hold of me
embraces me
tight
You don't want this
he says

Princess
I can see
you don't want this
you don't really want this
He says he loves me
He says I'm the one and only
He says he'll
hack me to shreds
if he has to
kill my mother
my brother
my father
set fire to our house
he says he loves me so much
that he'd have to kill himself
if I left him
This twitching mouth
this mad gleam in his eyes
I know what's coming
I want to get out the door
but my wrists
are cemented
in his grip
I head-butt his chin
feel his clenched fist
in my stomach
my breasts
in all the places
he normally strokes me

Doesn't look at me while he's doing this
Doesn't look at me
Doesn't look
Even when puke trickles from my mouth
and I scream like an animal
he still
doesn't
look

27 DON'T HEAR

Above the tracks.

(Silence.)

LEYLA: The guy I sprayed with –

MO: I know.

   (LEYLA is silent.)

   What about him?

LEYLA: It was –
   We were –

MO: I don't want to know.

LEYLA: He did things to me –

MO: I don't want to know!

LEYLA: He –

MO: Don't tell me!

LEYLA: Fuck you!

   (MO leaves.)

28 FIVE MINUTES

In front of the shed.

LEYLA: Arsehole.

MO: Leyla,
   I came back.

Five minutes later.
Five minutes later I was back.
But you'd gone

LEYLA: You came back?

MO: I've seen them Leyla. The bruises.
When you sat next to me, there was this naked bit of skin
between your trousers and your t-shirt,
and I could see.
I knew who'd done this too.
The guy who holds you tight
and sticks his tongue down your throat.
But at that moment – I just couldn't take it.
Five minutes later I came back.
And you'd gone.
Five minutes!
I stayed.
I hoped you'd –

I waited for you.
The whole night through.

29 BLACK AND BLUE

LEYLA, MOTHER, RICO.

RICO: She doesn't want to see you.

Are you deaf?
She doesn't want to see you.

Fuck off.
Leave us alone.

MOTHER: Where have you been.

(*LEYLA* is silent.)

Your boyfriend called.

LEYLA: I don't have a boyfriend.

MOTHER: He could actually talk.
        Wasn't as monosyllabic as most his age.
        Said he was worried sick about you.

LEYLA: Mum –

MO: Said you'd been so secretive lately.
        Distant.
        Impossible to reach.
        He kept asking me if you still loved him.
        He actually started crying down the phone.
        I felt really sorry for him.
        But what should I have said to comfort him?
        What do I know about you?

LEYLA: Mum –

(While mother talks LEYLA starts banging her head against the wall.)

MOTHER: He thinks you're cheating on him.
        Said you never want to tell him where you go.
        Never call him anymore.
        I know the feeling.
        I know it very well Leyla.

LEYLA: Mum –

MOTHER: I was surprised how much patience he has with you.
        You're lucky he's got such a big crush you.

(LEYLA bangs her head against the wall even harder.)

What are you doing?

(LEYLA continues.)

Stop it.
Stop this nonsense!

(LEYLA continues.)

Hey! Stop it!

(LEYLA continues.)

Leyla. Look at me.

(LEYLA continues.)

Stop this right now!

(LEYLA continues.)

RICO: It's ok mum, she's getting off on it,
it turns her on,
yes Leyla,
carry on,
yes,
yes –

MOTHER: Rico –

RICO: Harder,
So it bleeds,
come on, harder,
she's into SM –

MOTHER: Rico! Shut up!

RICO: You don't believe me?
Just look at her back.
You'll see for yourself.

(LEYLA continues.)

MOTHER: What's with your back?

(LEYLA continues.)

What's with your back Leyla?

*(LEYLA continues and keeps hitting her head harder
and harder against the wall. MOTHER goes towards her
and wants to pull her away. LEYLA hits her mother in
the face, till she loses balance and falls to the ground.
They look at each other. LEYLA lifts her t-shirt and
shows her back. It's covered in bruises.)*

LEYLA: My *boyfriend*. You talked to. Beats me black and blue.

(Silence.)

(*RICO* leaves.
MOTHER stands up, leaves and comes back with
disinfectant and bandages.)

MOTHER: Take it off.

(*MOTHER* gets a chair, *LEYLA* sits on it and takes off her t-shirt.
MOTHER begins to tend to her bruises. *LEYLA* suddenly
stands up.)

LEYLA: You think I'm disgusting.
The way you look at me
like a rotten piece of meat
which you have to force down
one mouthful after the other
force it
can't you see
you're going to puke in a minute

(*MOTHER* is silent.)

You should take a look at yourself mum,
you've got this fucking look on your face again.

(*LEYLA* leaves.
MOTHER cries without a sound.
RICO comes back and awkwardly tries to comfort
her.)

30 EYES

Above the tracks.

MO: If he touches you again
I'll kill him.

LEYLA: To me
he's already dead.

MO: I just can't believe you were together with someone
who'd do this to you.

LEYLA: It didn't happen straight away –

MO: But when it did you should've had the guts to –

LEYLA: Yes. I know.

MO: You let him control you!

LEYLA: Now I'm on my own.

MO: Your eyes. What's with your eyes?

LEYLA: Nothing.

MO: Have you put contacts in?

LEYLA: I thought you were colour-blind.

MO: It looks all misty.
        I can't see your eyes anymore.

LEYLA: Nobody has to see my eyes.
        My eyes are nobody's business.

31 GLITTER

Night.

MOTHER and LEYLA sit at the table.

LEYLA is deaf to her mother talking.

(Silence.)

MOTHER: When you were small I imagined this.
        The two of us sitting here with a glass of wine.
        Drinking.
        Talking.

        You'd be all sweaty from the disco
        and my neck would be stiff
        from sitting up late working on an article.
        I'd see what you'd experienced the moment you walk
        through the door.
        Not because of the love-bite
        (which you'd not even have noticed yet),

but because under your make-up your eyes are as round
and shiny
as when you were a small girl with a secret to tell me.
While you're chatting away I look at you.
Take everything in.
The glitter you put on your eyelids is smeared all over
your face.
Your face glistens like gift wrapping paper.
Your top seems far too tight, I still haven't got used to
your breasts.
And your perfume makes me dizzier than the wine.
Every now and then
I notice how your lips sometimes still miss each other
when the words tumble too hastily from your mouth.
Somehow this comforts me.
I see you in front of me, your lively features,
framed by your hair which is curly in front
and pressed flat at the back by the seat of the taxi.
I think:
This is my child.

I thought about this so often,
the two of us
in the middle of the night,
with a glass of wine.
I'm almost ashamed to say it,
but I was looking forward to it
before you could even say
mummy.

(Silence.)

32 NIGHT

In front of the shed. At some point it begins to rain softly.

LEYLA: I'm already in bed when Mo calls.
He wants to see me.

Says he can't sleep. There's a strange sound.
A rumbling in the background as if he's outside already.

MO: She says she'll come over right away.
Waiting in the rain seems like an eternity.
I'm afraid to climb onto the shed.
The wood is slippery and the wind far too strong.

LEYLA: Could you see anything?

MO: I had my torch.

LEYLA: Which you didn't switch on...

MO: I had to save the batteries. For later.

LEYLA: Normally I like the dark.
I feel as safe and cosy in it as he feels behind his
padlock.
But not today.
Today I have to make myself stop looking back
to see
if someone is following.

MO: I hear her coming and I see straight away
that she's not alone.

LEYLA: A light flashes by my head.
I thought it was you.

MO: He hits her in the face. Stares at her. Not a word.
She doesn't move. Not a flicker.
He hurls himself at her feet.
Whimpers. Drivels.
Begs. Weeps.
Kisses her feet.
It's like he's done this a hundred times before.
She just stands there,
still,
upright
and lets him do it.

LEYLA: I look into his eyes.
A whipped dog asking his master to forgive him.
To be loved again.
Stroked again?

No
Thrashed.
My eyes. His eyes.
I look at him from very far away.
Study him.
And study myself, the way I'm standing here,
his face staring up at me
and I see how
his face disgusts me.

MO: She puts her hands on his shoulders.
Grips them firmly. And pushes him away.
Very slowly. Without a word.
She turns around
and steps into the dark.

He gets up
grabs her by the neck and pulls her back.
Like in the club.
This time I don't hide.

LEYLA: I try to break away from his tight grip.
He only lets go once Mo appears and pushes him off.
BULL just stares at him.
A leopard seizing up a lamb.
He's going to eat him alive, I think.
I want to scream out
but it's too late
he grabs Mo and smashes him against the shed.

MO: My head hits wood,
I hear a thud,
hear it again and again and again.
High above me I see the lamps over the tracks
bobbing up and down in the same rhythm
like little dots of light in the sky
getting blurrier and blurrier
and suddenly it's as if I'm diving down
into a pool of deep, black water.

LEYLA: BULL loses it,

his fists go manic,
he wants to smash Mo up,
punch him to pulp,
crush his cheekbone.

I grab him, pound at him, scream in his face,
beg him to stop
but he just beats harder.

Mo –
Is he still alive –

I have to,
I have to do something,
anything,
quick –

my brain is empty and silent,
empty and silent,
all at once everything has evaporated into thin air,
floats away as a cloud,
high up where I can't reach it,
a castle in the clouds,
my brain,
every thought vanishes inside it,
all I see is Mo
and above him BULL
and I know that he will continue
until –

I blindly grab out,
clutch something,
bring it down on BULL's head,
as hard as I can.

He winces,
turns around and looks me in the eye,
with a stare that fills me with terror.

His mouth forms words,
but I don't hear what he's saying,
I can only think of Mo,
and that he's let go of him.

His fist comes at me,
hits me hard on the chin,
I stumble,
the ground beneath me slides away.

Mo!

At the beginning sparks flew.

MO: Sparks?

LEYLA: Yeah. Sparks.

MO: You mean fists.
Fists flew.

LEYLA: I asked him what his name was.

MO: Mo.

LEYLA: What kind of a name's that?

33 OR 0

MO: I made it up myself. Mo.

LEYLA: What?
And your real name? What's your real name?

(Pause.)

MO: Leyla. It's raining.

*(Pause. **LEYLA** and **MO** awaken to the present.)*

LEYLA: Where is BULL?

(Pause.)

Gone.

THE END